ARMY OFFICER SELECTION BOARD (AOSB)

www.How2Become.com

Orders: Please contact How2become Ltd, Suite 1, 60 Churchill Square Business Centre, Kings Hill, Kent ME19 4YU. You can also order via the e mail address info@how2become.com.

ISBN: 9781910602546

First published in 2010 by How2Become Ltd.

Updated in 2019.

Typeset for How2become Ltd by Gemma Butler

Printed in Great Britain for How2become Ltd by CMP.

Disclaimer

Do you want to attend a 1 Day Army Officer AOSB preparation training course?

Visit the following website to find out more:

ARMYOFFICERCOURSE.CO.UK

CONTENTS

Chapter 1 The Qualities Required to Become an Army Officer 9

Chapter 2 The Selection Process for Becoming an Army Officer 15

Chapter 3 The Army Officer Scoring Criteria 33

Chapter 4 The Army Careers Advisor (ACA) Interview 45

Chapter 5 The Command Tasks and Obstacle Course 69

Chapter 6 Preparing for the Planning Exercise 75

Chapter 7 How to Pass the AOSB Interviews 97

Chapter 8 Sample Numerical, Verbal & Abstract Reasoning Tests ... 105

A Few Final Words 175

Welcome to your new guide – *How to Pass the Army Officer Selection Board.* This guide has been designed to help you prepare for, and pass the Army Officer selection process, including the Army Officer Selection Board (AOSB).

The founder of How2become, Richard McMunn, has spent over 20 years in both the Armed Forces and the Emergency Services. He has vast experience and knowledge in the area of Armed Forces recruitment and you will find his guide both inspiring and highly informative. During his successful career in the Fire Service, Richard sat on many interview panels, assessing applicants applying to join the Fire Service. He has also been extremely successful at passing job interviews and assessments himself, and has a success rate of over 90%. Follow his advice and preparation techniques carefully and you too can achieve the same levels of success in your career.

Whilst the selection process for joining the Army as an Officer is highly competitive, there are a number of things you can do in order to improve your chances of success, and they are all contained within this guide.

The guide itself has been split up into useful sections to make it easier for you to prepare for each stage. Read each section carefully and take notes as you progress. Don't ever give up on your dreams; if you really want to become an Army Officer then you can do it. The way to prepare for a job in the Armed Forces as an Officer is to embark on a programme of 'in-depth' preparation, and this guide will show you exactly how to do just that.

If you need any further help with the Army Officer Selection tests, Planning Exercises, getting fit or Army Officer Interview advice, then we offer a wide range of courses, books and DVD products to assist you. These are all available through our online shop www.How2Become.com.

We are also now running a number of 1 Day Army Officer Selection Board preparation training courses at the following link: ArmyOfficerCourse.co.uk

Once again, thank you for your custom and we wish you every success in your pursuit of joining the Army as an Officer.

Work hard, stay focused, and secure your dream career...

Sincerely,

The how2become team

The How2Become Team

PREFACE

BY RICHARD MCMUNN

I spent four years in the Armed Forces, from the age of 17 to 21. During these four years I experienced some of the best moments of my life. My career in the Armed Forces taught me how to be disciplined, it taught me how to be organised, and it also provided me with a sound footing for a successful future. But it didn't start out all plain sailing. I initially failed the selection process for the Armed Forces, at the medical stage, as I was overweight.

I can remember sitting in the Armed Forces careers office in Preston, Lancashire at the age of 16. I had waited patiently to see the Warrant Officer, who would interview me as part of my application for joining. I had already passed the written tests, and despite never having sat an interview before in my life, I was confident of success. In the build up to the interview I had worked very hard studying the position I was applying for, and also working on my interview technique. At the end of the interview I was told that I had easily passed and all that was left to complete was the medical. While I was delighted with this, in the back of my mind, there was a slight doubt. I knew that I was overweight, and that this could cause an issue. At the medical, my fears became a reality. I was told by the doctor that I would have to lose a stone in weight before they would accept me. I walked out of the doctor's surgery, towards the bus stop that would take me back home, three miles away. I was absolutely gutted, and embarrassed. I had failed at the final hurdle, all because I was overweight!

So, there I was, sitting at the bus stop feeling sorry for myself, and wondering what job I was going to apply for next. My dream of joining the Armed Forces was over. I didn't know which way to turn. Suddenly, I began to feel a sense of determination to lose the weight and get fit in the shortest time possible. It was at that particular point in my life when things would change forever. As the bus approached I remember thinking there was no time like the present for getting started on my fitness regime. I therefore opted to walk the three miles home instead of being lazy and getting the bus. When I got home I sat in my room and wrote out a 'plan of action' that would dictate how I was going to lose the weight required. That plan of action was very simple, and it said the following three things:

1. Every weekday morning I will get up at 6am and run 3 miles.
2. Instead of catching the bus to college, and then back home again, I will walk.
3. I will eat healthily, and I will not go over the recommended daily calorific intake.

Every day I would read my simple 'action plan' and it acted as a reminder of what I needed to do. Within a few weeks of following my plan rigidly I had lost over a stone in weight and I was a lot fitter too! When I returned back to the doctor's surgery for my medical the doctor was amazed that I had managed to lose the weight in such a short space of time and he was pleased that I had been so determined to pass the medical. Six months later I started my basic training course with a big smile on my face!

Ever since then I have always made sure that I prepare properly for any job application. If I do fail a particular interview or section of an application process then I will always go out of my way to ask for feedback so that I can improve for next time. I also still use an 'action plan' in just about every element of my work today. Action plans allow you to focus your mind on what you want to achieve and I would strongly recommend that you use one during your preparation for the Army Officer Selection process.

Throughout my career I have always been successful. It's not because I am better than the next person, but simply because I prepare better. I didn't do very well at school so I have to work a lot harder to pass the exams and written tests that form part of a job application process, but I am always aware of what I need to do and what I must improve on.

I have always been a great believer in preparation. Preparation was my key to success, and will also be yours. Without the right level of preparation you will be setting out on the route to failure. The Army is hard to join as an Officer, but if you follow the steps that I have compiled within this guide and use them as part of your preparation, then you will increase your chances of success dramatically.

The men and women of the Armed Forces carry out an amazing job. They are there to protect us and our country and they do that job with great pride, passion and very high levels of professionalism and commitment. They are to be congratulated for the job that they do. Before you apply to join the Army as an Officer you need to be fully confident that you too are capable of providing that same level of commitment. If you think you can do it, and you can rise to the challenge, then you just might be the type of person the Army is looking for.

Best wishes,

Richard McMunn

CHAPTER 1
THE QUALITIES REQUIRED TO BECOME AN ARMY OFFICER

Before getting into the selection process and the different elements of the Army Officer Selection Board, we will go into detail about the qualities that are required to become an Army Officer. The reason for this is simple: we want you to concentrate on demonstrating these throughout the duration of the selection process. If you demonstrate these then your chances of success will increase dramatically.

Many candidates who attend the AOSB will be under prepared. In addition to this, many candidates will spend hours scouring internet chat forums in an attempt to find hints and tips on how to pass the AOSB. Whilst there is nothing wrong with this, the most effectively prepared candidates are those who concentrate primarily on demonstrating the key assessable qualities in order to become an Army Officer.

The whole purpose of the AOSB is to determine whether or not you have the 'potential' to become an Army Officer. If you have the potential then there is a greater chance that you will pass the Officer Initial Training course at Sandhurst. The Army will be investing literally hundreds of thousands of pounds into your development and career progression. Therefore, they want to be sure that you have the potential to pass every stage of training.

In order to assess your potential, the Army will assess you against a series of qualities and competencies. Before moving on to the scoring criteria we shall talk a little about the qualities that you need to demonstrate during the entire selection process. You will notice that after each list of qualities we have provided you with some useful tips.

Qualities that you need to demonstrate:

- Determination
- Resolute
- Persistent
- Unwavering
- Steady
- Able to overcome most difficulties
- Strong-willed

TIPS: You are applying to join the Army as an Officer. Therefore, it is crucial that you are able to remain calm in a crisis, be totally focused on achieving the end result, and be determined to succeed at everything you do.

For example, during the planning exercise stage, which is probably the toughest part of the AOSB, you will be placed under considerable pressure by the assessing Officers. If you do not know the answer to a question then it is better to say so, rather than panic, waffle or crumble under the pressure. One of the main purposes of AOSB is to determine whether or not you have the ability to stay focused under pressure.

- Imaginative
- Initiative
- Constructive
- Perceptive
- Original
- Mentally agile
- Inventive
- Visionary
- Intelligent
- Mature
- Balanced

TIPS: These qualities are predominantly focused on your state of mind. Do you have the ability to come up with solutions to problems? Can you think outside the box? Can you see the end result? Are you sensible and mature for your years? During every stage of the AOSB make sure you remain level-headed. Do not act in a foolhardy way and always think before you speak. Engage your brain before you engage your mouth!

- Forceful
- Compelling
- Persuasive
- Powerful
- Vigorous
- Assertive
- Consistent
- Effective
- Resourceful
- Magnetic
- Inspiring
- Considerate
- Considerable impact

TIPS: Let us assume that you are participating in the Planning Exercise phase. You have worked hard during your preparation in the build up to AOSB and you are very confident that your plan of tackling the exercise is the most effective. However, two other members of your group have alternative solutions to the problem. What do you do? The options are simple – you can either go along with their desired solution(s) or you can have the confidence in your own abilities and your plan and attempt to 'persuade' them both that your option is the most effective. When attending AOSB, you should have the confidence in your own abilities and persuade them that you have the most effective option.

Remember – you are applying to become an Army Officer and that means you are applying to become a leader!

- Bold
- Daring
- Courageous
- Entrepreneurial
- Enthusiastic
- Spirit of adventure
- Untiring
- Energetic
- Active
- Diligent
- Industrious
- Persevering
- Physically strong and active
- Organiser
- Sense of urgency.

TIPS: During Command Tasks be sure to get involved. Those people who believe that if they sit on the fence and don't get involved will go unnoticed, are sorely mistaken. You must get involved, come up with solutions, encourage the team, support others and try your hardest to achieve every task that you are set. When it is your turn to take command, do so. Do not be weak; be strong, confident and in control at all times; more on this later.

- Tolerant
- Flexible
- Co-operative
- Diplomatic
- Tactful
- Resilient (never gives in)
- Adaptable
- Willing to accept responsibility.

TIPS: What are you like towards other people? Do you have the ability to work with others as part of a team? Every team encounters problems along the way. How you deal with those problems is what matters. Be tolerant of other people, always be flexible in your approach to tasks, never give in and be the first to put your hand up when they ask for a volunteer.

- Sensible
- Respective
- Shrewd
- Well-balanced
- Decisive
- Discerning
- Fair
- Unbiased
- Loyal
- Steadfast

You have now been provided with plenty of qualities that all go towards making an effective Army Officer. So, when the interview panel asks you the question "What are the qualities of an Army Officer?" you will have no problem answering it!

Army Officers are both **leaders** and **managers**. Therefore, it is important that you understand the difference between each of them and how they are interlinked.

In order to become a competent Army Officer you will need to be effective at both. Here's a brief explanation of how they differ:

Leader – A leader is someone who effectively takes a team of people from point A to point B. These two 'points' don't have to be in terms of distance, but instead they could be a mission, a company, or organisational goal. For example, a football manager attempting to lead his or her team to promotion to a higher league. A leader should be a visionary. They should 'see' where they want their team to be and take steps to get them there.

Manager – A manager is someone who arranges and uses resources in order to achieve a company's or organisation's goal. Examples of resources are:

- People
- Utilities such as water, gas and electricity
- Vehicles and equipment
- Paper and pencils
- Fuel
- Time

An effective manager will use his or her resources effectively. They will not waste resources and they will use them appropriately. A manager's greatest asset is the people whom they command. When you join the Army as an Officer you will undoubtedly be responsible at some point in your career for a group or team of people. How you manage them is very important.

Being an officer in the Army is about drawing on different skills and assets in order to achieve a task or goal. That goal may take many years to achieve and may not necessarily be a short-term objective. Always remember that in order to become a competent Army Officer, you will need to be an effective leader and manager.

CHAPTER 2
THE SELECTION PROCESS FOR BECOMING AN ARMY OFFICER

The majority of people who read this guide will have a thorough understanding of what the Army Officer Selection process consists of. Before getting into each element of selection, and more importantly how to pass it, it is important to briefly explain the different elements.

To begin with, applicants will need to contact their local Armed Forces Careers Office and explain that they wish to apply to become an Officer with the British Army. The most effective way to do this is to go along to your nearest centre for a brief chat. You will be supplied with an information pack and details on how to apply, providing you meet the minimum eligibility requirements. You can also research the different jobs that are available as an officer by using the Army's online job explorer. This can be found by visiting the Army website at: army.mod.uk

THE ARMY CAREERS ADVISOR INTERVIEW

You will eventually be invited to attend what is called the Army Careers Advisor (ACA) interview. Sometimes this interview is referred to as the AFCO interview or the 'filter' interview. This interview is designed to assess whether or not you have the right qualities to become an Army Officer and it is also the opportunity for you to decide whether or not the Army is for you. If you successfully pass the ACA interview and a medical check, you will be put forward to attend the Army Officer Selection Board briefing. The ACA interview is, in my opinion, relatively easy to pass. However, you will still need to put in plenty of preparation and I have provided you with a host of sample questions and responses during a later section of this guide. In order to successfully become an Army Officer you will need to pass two boards. The first is an AOSB briefing and the second is the Main Board.

THE AOSB BRIEFING

The AOSB briefing is 2 days in duration and is held at the Westbury. During your stay here you will be assessed on:

1. Your physical ability;
2. Practical ability;
3. Teamwork ability;
4. Leadership ability.

The briefing is also an opportunity for you to see whether Army life is for you and to also prepare for the full AOSB Main Board. During the briefing you will get to try many of the elements that you'll be assessed against during the Main Board, such as:

- An opening discussion with the other candidates
- Aptitude tests – Verbal Reasoning, Numerical Reasoning and Abstract Reasoning. In this guide we have included a chapter with sample Numerical, Verbal and Abstract Reasoning tests.
- Planning exercise
- Practical techniques
- Physical fitness tests including the bleep test and an obstacle course

The obstacle course itself consists of five elements: A high wall, 2 hurdles, long jump, rope swing and walking up barred steps whilst carrying an object. You only have to go around the course once and you are allowed three attempts at each obstacle.

The Bleep Test is stopped when you have reached the required level 10.2 for men and 8.1 for women. I have provided you with lots of free resources to assist you for the aptitude tests at the following link: ArmyOfficerTests.co.uk

Once the briefing is complete the assessors will get together and discuss your performance. You will be placed in one of the four categories:

CATEGORY 1 – Invited to attend the AOSB Main Board.

CATEGORY 2 – You will be invited to attend AOSB Main Board after a set period of time during which you will be required to work on your weaker areas.

CATEGORY 3 – The board believes that you will fail Main Board. However, you can attend if you wish to do so.

CATEGORY 4 – Unsuitable for AOSB Main Board.

As you can see, it is important to aim for CATEGORY 1 or CATEGORY 2 at the very least. If you achieve CATEGORY 1 then you will normally be invited back to Westbury within 8 weeks. During this 8-week period it is vital that you continue your preparation. Passing the briefing is by no means an indication that you will pass the Main Board.

THE AOSB MAIN BOARD

The AOSB Main Board takes place at Westbury. Boards usually run during the week, however, there are weekend boards for those people who cannot genuinely attend during the week.

At each Main Board there will normally be up to 40 people attending, both male and female. You will be split up into medium sized groups of approximately 8 people for the duration of the board. Groups will consist of men and women of a variety of different ages. This is done deliberately, to assess whether or not you can work with people of the opposite sex and also with people whom are younger and older than you.

You will be assessed against a number of different areas, which will be explained later in the guide.

The AOSB Main Board is designed to assess whether or not you have the right personal qualities and attributes to become a successful Army Officer. The only way you will pass it is through hard work and determination.

There are two key elements to passing the AOSB –

1. How you perform
2. How you behave

Whilst there are many different factors that can influence each element, they both must be taken seriously. For example, you will be required to work in groups of up to 8 people. How you treat each member of your group, both as a team player and a team leader, will be assessed. You will also be assessed on your attitude. If you are cocky, arrogant, dismissive, or you have a negative attitude towards discipline, then you will not pass the board.

The assessors will naturally expect you to have found out as much as you can about the Army, its history, its mission, its equipment, weapons, tanks and aircraft, and they will also ask you questions about the training you would expect to go through if you are successful both as an officer and as part of your chosen trade/branch. There is plenty of hard work ahead of you if you want to pass the AOSB Main Board, but the hard work will certainly be worth it!

During the Main Board you will be required to undergo the following key assessable areas:

DAY 1

Fitness tests: These will be carried out shortly after you arrive at the AOSB and you will be required to undertake the bleep test, the exact same test as the briefing. Males are expected to achieve level 10.2 and females 8.1. If you fail to achieve the minimum standard then it is highly likely that you will be asked to leave the board. Anyone who cannot reach this standard before they arrive at board is, in our opinion, underprepared. You know before you attend the Main Board what the standard is, therefore you should be able to achieve it with great ease. If you do not have a copy of the bleep test then you can obtain one right now at: How2Become.com Do not leave it until the last minute to reach the required fitness level, start working on your fitness now.

Essay and General Knowledge tests: Following the brief by the assessing staff you will be required to write an essay based on a specific topic that is usually centered on current affairs. Many people score poorly on the written essay, simply because they fail to put in any practice before the main board.

Following the essay, you will be required to sit the following computer-based tests:

- General knowledge
- Army/Service knowledge
- Current affairs

In our opinion the Army/Service knowledge test questions can be prepared for. However, the general knowledge questions that you will encounter from the test will be extremely diverse in nature. We are not saying that you shouldn't prepare for this part of the test, however it is our belief that you should spend more time concentrating on the other two elements during your preparation time.

EXAMPLES OF ARMY/SERVICE KNOWLEDGE QUESTIONS

As part of your preparation, go away and find out the answer to each of the following questions.

1. Troops fighting on the front line are issued with CBA. What does CBA stand for?

2. What is the rank badge of Staff Sergeant?

3. The L129A1 Sharpshooter rifle fires what size round?

4. Which insignia denotes a Lieutenant General?

5. What does N.A.T.O stand for?

6. How much is the annual Army Budget?

7. What is the highest commissioned rank of the Army?

8. What is the highest non-commissioned rank of the Army?

9. The Mk 6 Assault Boat is constructed from what metal?

10. The Combat Support Boat is used exclusively by which Corps?

11. How many countries are in NATO?

12. Name all of the UK Army bases?

13. What is the name of the military operations in Afghanistan?

14. What is the purpose of the Army's Logistic Vehicles?

15. The ATMP is a versatile, lightweight load-carrying vehicle used by airborne and air-mobile battalions. What does ATMP stand for?

16. DROPS vehicles form the logistic backbone of the British Army. What does DROPS stand for?

17. Name 5 types of Protected Patrol Vehicles?

18. How many Army personnel are there approximately?

19. The Defender is the latest version of the Islander twin turboprop aircraft. What is its gross weight?

20. What is the maximum speed in knots of the Gazelle helicopter?

21. What does CBRN stand for?

22. The Light Role Team (LRT) Is the United Kingdom's early entry capability for CBRN. They provide Detection, Identification, Monitoring and what two other functions?

23. Who is the current Commander-in-Chief Land Forces?

24. The Commander-in-Chief Land Forces reports directly to whom?

25. The Starstreak HVM is designed to counter threats from very high performance, low-flying aircraft. What does HVM stand for?

26. The Rapier Field Standard C is a technologically advanced SHORAD. What does SHORAD stand for?

27. Officer Initial Training takes place where?

28. The Commissioning Course for Regular Army Officers, including recess periods, is how long?

29. The GMLRS provides pinpoint accuracy delivering a 200lb high explosive warhead to its target. What does GMLRS stand for?

30. Who is the current Chief of the General Staff?

The above 30 questions are just a small sample of the type of question you will encounter. Try to spend plenty of time studying the Army website during your preparation. Not only will this help you during the computer-based tests but it will also assist you during the interviews. We would also recommend you obtain a copy of the following book from Amazon and all good bookstores as it contains a wealth of information relating to the British Army – *The British Army: A Pocket Guide*

ESSAY WRITING TIPS

1. For the introduction, write the thesis statement and give some background information. The thesis statement is put into the essay introduction and it should reveal your point of view on the matter, or the position you intend to support in your paper.
2. Develop each supporting paragraph and make sure to follow the correct format.
3. Write clear and simple sentences to express your meaning.
4. Focus on the main idea of your essay.
5. Consider using a well-structured format for you essay such as: Beginning – Include the thesis statement and background information. Middle – This will be the main part of the essay and will include your argument, the reasons for it and any supporting evidence or information. End – Conclude and summarise.

Try writing an essay on any of the following topics:

1. Politicians too often base their decisions on what will please the voters, not on what is best for the country.
2. Wealthy politicians cannot offer fair representation to all the people.
3. In a free society, laws must be subject to change.
4. An understanding of the past is necessary for solving the problems of the present.
5. Education comes not from books but from practical experience.
6. Is climate change man-made?
7. Should the death penalty be re-introduced?
8. Is the current electoral system fair?
9. Is torture ever acceptable in today's world?
10. Is it right that men should get paternity leave from work?
11. Is the UK taxation system fair?
12. Are we too reliant on computers and the internet?
13. Should we use animals for research?
14. Should the UK government have a say in what we eat and drink?
15. Does access to condoms prevent teenage pregnancy and sexually transmitted diseases?

On completion of the essay exercise, you will also be required to sit Mental Aptitude tests, Memory & Attention test, and a Personality test. The Mental Aptitude tests are similar to the tests you will sit at the briefing. Sample tests are provided in this guide.

MEMORY AND ATTENTION TEST

The scope of the Memory and Attention Test is to assess the speed at which candidates memorise instructions and how accurately they are applied. The test itself lasts for twenty minutes and the difficulty and number of instructions per question increases as the test progresses. The results are used to analyse the candidate's pattern of responses and create a profile. The different areas analysed are as follows.

- Speed of working – The overall time taken to finish the test.
- Memory – the amount of times candidate's need to refresh their memory regarding the current set of instructions.
- Accuracy – the number of test questions that are completed correctly in regards to the corresponding instructions.

THE AOSB PERSONALITY ASSESSMENT

The personality assessment is taken on a computer and has two hundred questions in total. The average time to complete the test is between 30-40 minutes. The test provides the assessors with an idea of a candidate's personality. In this test there are no right or wrong answers, and you should answer the questions honestly. It will not help the candidate if they try to answer in the way they believe the AOSB wants to hear. The system is designed so any inconsistencies are highlighted in the results.

DAY 2

The Opening Discussion: At the beginning of day 2 you will be required to undertake a group discussion. This part of the assessment will last for approximately 40 minutes, during which time you will be required to discuss a number of different topics with the other members of your group. The most effective way to prepare for this part of the AOSB is to:

1. Have an excellent knowledge of current affairs

2. Be a good communicator verbally

3. Be a good listener

The group opening discussion element of the AOSB is designed to assess your ability to communicate and interact with other people. As you are already aware, Army Officers are required to communicate, and discuss topical issues with other members of the Army. In addition to this they must have the intellect to converse with agencies outside of the Armed Forces as well as their colleagues from the RAF and the Royal Navy. This part of the assessment will determine your ability to do just that.

There will be up to eight people in the discussion, all of whom will be a mix of ages and genders. It is important that you can get on with everyone, regardless of their age, background, religious beliefs or sexual orientation. Before we provide you with some tips on how to score high during the group opening discussion, let us first take a look at three important assessable areas:

- Confidence and Resilience
- Oral Communication
- Influence

Many candidates believe that all you need to do during the discussion in order to score well is to contribute. This couldn't be further from the truth. Yes, it is imperative that you get involved and have an opinion, but you must concentrate on other areas too, such as your ability to listen to others and involve others in the conversation. You will see that one of the assessable areas is that of 'influence'. During the discussion, you may be presented with a situation where the other members of the group disagree with your opinion or view. Whilst that is fine and acceptable, would you be able to influence them and change their mind about your views?

Here are a number of important tips that will help you score high during the group discussion.

Tip 1

Whilst in the chair, sit upright and do not slouch or lean forward. Sit with your legs uncrossed and rest your palms on your knees. Whilst you should not sit rigid, you should look presentable.

Tip 2

There will be a number of discussions to be had. In total the discussion session will last for approximately 40 minutes, so there is ample time for you to get involved and score high. Try starting off a few discussions. Don't just leave it to the other members of the group to start off the topic. Remember, one of the assessable areas is that of confidence and resilience.

If you are struggling to think of anything to say for a specific topic, you could start off the conversation by saying:

"Does anybody have any strong views on this topic?"

By saying this, you will be actively involved in the conversation and you will be also involving others in the conversation.

Tip 3

When you have finished contributing to the debate, try and involve another person in the conversation. For example:

"That's my view on this subject, what do you think?"

Once again you will score higher marks for actively involving others in the conversation.

Tip 4

Involve other people who have not yet had chance to speak. If you notice a member of the group struggling to get their opinion heard, try saying something like:

"I notice you haven't had the chance to say anything yet, what's your view on this subject?"

Tip 5

Actively demonstrate good listening skills. This is the part that many people are poor at. Once they have finished speaking, they sit back and wait for their turn to speak again. Avoid this at all costs! We strongly recommend that you show active listening skills when other people in the group are speaking. Nod your head and use facial expressions to demonstrate that you are still involved in the topic of conversation.

Tip 6

Be careful what you say! Over the past few years we have run a number of 1-day Army Officer training courses that help people prepare for their AOSB. During the course we go through a number of group opening discussions. During every session, someone is guaranteed to say something that will probably give them an automatic fail for the entire AOSB! Sometimes people have a tendency to say something controversial; albeit they probably didn't intend to. Our advice is this – it is important that you get involved during the discussions, and even more important that you have an opinion and don't sit on the fence. However, you must think before you speak. If you believe that what you will say might be taken in the wrong way, avoid saying it.

Tip 7

Speak clearly and concisely. During the group opening discussion be clear in what you say, speak up and avoid hesitations such as 'erm' or 'umm'. In addition to other areas, you are being assessed on your oral communication skills.

Tip 8

Have a number of topics that you can start off a discussion with. Although it is more probable that the assessing staff will provide you the topics to discuss, they may also ask you to come up with topics yourself. Therefore, before you attend AOSB, pick 5 subjects that you can use during the group discussions phase.

Now let's take a look at a number of sample topics that have been used in the past.

SAMPLE GROUP DISCUSSION TOPICS

- Should women be allowed to join the Armed Forces?
- Was Hitler a good leader?
- What do you think about gay people being allowed to join the Armed Forces?
- Speeding cameras are a total waste of time – discuss.
- How could the use and popularity of public transport be increased within this country?
- Professional footballers. Are they overpaid?
- Is the increase in overseas football club owners good for the sport? The pros and cons of having a credit card.
- Marijuana has a medical value.
- The pros and cons of a female President.
- Should schools distribute condoms?
- Life imprisonment is a good alternative to capital punishment. What makes a good leader?
- Was the Iraq war a waste of time?
- What should Britain's place in Europe be?
- Is modern technology changing the way we communicate for the better? Should smoking have been banned in public places?
- Is animal testing defensible in modern society?
- Should the public be concerned about the increasing use of DNA technology?
- Should people be required to opt out of organ donation rather than opt in? How could more people be encouraged to vote?
- Can the salaries of professional football players be justified? Should the private life of celebrities come under so much scrutiny?
- Do we need to change the attitude of car drivers towards speed limits? Should our police officers be routinely armed?
- Should we be worried about obesity?
- Should organised team sport be included in the national curriculum? Should there be a compulsory retirement age?

- Do we need to change Britain's drinking culture?
- Should there be any limitations to the treatment available on the NHS? Has the National Lottery been good for Britain?
- Should the BBC be funded by a license fee?

Numerous interviews All candidates who attend the AOSB Main Board will be required to sit interviews with the Vice President, Deputy President and Education Adviser.

We have dedicated an entire section to the AOSB interviews in a later section of this guide.

Outdoor tasks: The outdoor tasks are normally carried out after lunch on the second day. Therefore, it is important that you don't eat a 'heavy' meal. Eat something that is packed full of carbohydrates and also remember to drink plenty of water.

The outdoor task is basically a 'leaderless' task, which means there is no designated leader. An example of a task might be where you are required to get from point A to B without touching the floor and whilst carrying a heavy object such as a large metal drum or heavy ammunition box.

Once again, we have dedicated a chapter to the outdoor tasks later on in this guide.

Once the outdoor task is complete you will be required to compete against the other groups in a leaderless task. During this part of the assessment, which is called the opening race, you will be assessed against your overall effort, teamwork ability, potential leadership and problem-solving skills.

Planning exercise tutorial: The final part of the second day will see you receive a planning exercise tutorial in preparation for the following day's assessment. As previously mentioned, it is my personal belief that the Planning Exercise is the hardest part of the entire AOSB. We have dedicated an entire section of this guide to the Planning Exercise.

DAY 3

Planning exercise: At the commencement of day 3 you will be required to take part in the planning exercise. This is a theoretical written exercise which will assess your ability to use time, resources and people in an effective and efficient manner. You will be provided with a written brief relating to a fictitious scenario. You will also be provided with a map to study that is relative to the brief. You will have an hour to read, study and analyse the brief, and come up with your own solution to the problem. Once the hour is complete, you will then be required to discuss the scenario with your group in order to come up with an agreed solution to the problem.

You will be assessed against how you contribute to the discussion and also how you react to the ideas of others within your group.

Once the group discussion element is complete, you will be required to answer questions on your decisions by the assessing officers.

Outdoor Command tasks: Following the planning exercise stage you will then be required to take command of a group of people. When it is not your turn to be in command, you will be required to act as a team member. The leader of the group will brief you and then allow you just a few minutes to develop your plan. You will then be required to explain the plan to your group before executing it.

Once again we have dedicated an entire section to the outdoor command task in a later chapter of this guide.

Obstacle course: The final task of the morning on day three is the individual obstacle course. You will be required to negotiate an obstacle course with the object of completing as many obstacles as possible within a set time limit.

Lecturette: In the afternoon of day 3 you will be required to give a 5-minute talk to the rest of the group on a subject that is chosen from your CV. You will have 5 subjects to choose from and you will be given a set time period to prepare. However, it is our strong advice that you study your CV and practice giving a presentation, before you attend the AOSB. Once the 5-minute period is complete you will then be required to answer questions from your group. The lecturette is designed to assess your ability and confidence when talking in front of a group of people.

Dinner: In the evening of day 3 you will enjoy a formal dinner the rest of the candidates. Whilst the Army will tell you that this activity is not assessed, remember that they will not score your performance until the following day. Don't get drunk, don't show off and don't make a fool of yourself!

DAY 4

Final race: During the morning of the final day you will take part in what is called the final race. This is an outdoor leaderless task that will see your group go up against the other groups in a race to finish an obstacle course. This is your final chance to really show the assessing officers how good you are.

Immediately following the final race the board will meet up to discuss your performance. The board take this part extremely seriously and the comments made by the Group Leader, the Deputy President, and the Education Adviser will be analysed and discussed in depth. The results of your board will be sent out to you that day and will normally take just 2-3 days to arrive.

Now that we understand what the selection process consists of, let's take a look at the scoring criteria.

CHAPTER 3
THE ARMY OFFICER SCORING CRITERIA

Within this section of the guide we will provide you with information that relates to how the Army will assess you during the entire officer selection process. During the second section of this chapter we will provide you with information that is relative to the AOSB scoring criteria.

The criteria that we are going to provide you with during this first section relates to your own personal attributes, qualities and also your knowledge of the Army and your chosen career as an officer. This information will act as a very good foundation for your preparation and you should learn it before you attend the initial ACA interview. If you are capable of providing the Army selecting officers with what they are looking for, then your chances of success will greatly increase.

The marking sheet used to assess your abilities covers a number of different assessable areas. The following list is a selection of some of the criteria used:

- Personal turnout;
- Sociability;
- Emotional maturity and stability;
- Drive and determination to succeed;
- Physically robust;
- Experience of being self-reliant;
- Reactions to social discipline;
- Experience of and reaction to regimentation and routine;
- Knowledge and experience of Army life;
- Motivation to join the Army;
- Reasons for wanting to join an officer;
- Experience of leadership;
- Personal circumstances.

This list is not exhaustive and there will be other areas that the Army will be assessing you on during the initial ACA interview. However, having an understanding of the qualities you need to demonstrate throughout selection will improve your chances of success dramatically.

In order to provide you with a greater understanding of what is required we will now go into more detail about each specific area.

PERSONAL TURNOUT

The Army are looking for you to be smartly dressed when you attend the AFCO. Try to think of how you would expect an Army Officer to present themselves. You would expect them to be smart, formal and professional. When you attend the careers office, whether it is for an interview or a careers presentation, always make sure you wear a formal outfit such as a suit or shirt and tie. Whilst this is not essential, it will allow you to score higher in the area of 'personal turnout'.

Many people will stroll into the careers office wearing jeans and trainers. Make an effort to stand out for the right reasons and this certainly will work in your favour. Those people who turn up to the Armed Forces Careers Office dressed untidy and unwashed will score poorly.

Tips for scoring high in personal turnout:

- Make sure your shoes are clean and polished;
- Shirt, trousers and tie for males, and a smart formal outfit for females;
- Ensure your clothes are ironed and not creased;
- Work on your personal hygiene and overall appearance. Make sure your nails are clean!
- Stand tall and be confident;
- Don't slouch in the interview chair.

SOCIABILITY

This section assesses your ability to mix well with people. The Army want to know that you are socially confident and outgoing. It is also important that you have a good sense of humour. They want to know that you can fit in well with the Army way of life and that you have no problems with communal living.

When you join the Army you will be required to live in accommodation with other people. Some people find it very difficult to socialise with others and these are not the type of people the Army want to recruit, especially as officers. They need people who will fit into the team spirit and whom have no problem with communicating with others. Those applicants who come across as quiet or shy will not score well in the area of sociability. At no point during selection should you be brash, abrasive or not a team player.

Tips for scoring high in sociability:

- During the interviews, provide examples of where you have mixed well with others. This may be through your current work position of with youth organisations such as the Scouts etc;

- If you have played team sports then this will be an advantage;
- Tell the interviewer that you will have no problem with communal living. Communal living is living with other people. During your Officer Initial Training you will be required to live in a room with other student officers, so the Army want to know that you are comfortable with this;
- Smile and laugh where appropriate – a sense of humour is a must but never be overbearing or over confident. Never 'back chat' or be disrespectful to the recruiting officers and staff.

EMOTIONAL MATURITY AND STABILITY

The Army want to see that you are mature for your age and that you are even tempered and well balanced. This is especially important when applying to join as an Officer. They don't want people who are aggressive or who come across as having a bad attitude. They want to see that you have coped well with the ups and downs of life so far, and you may find that they ask you questions on any difficult areas of life that you have had to deal with. They want to know that you will adapt well to the change in lifestyle when you join the Army and that you can cope in highly stressful situations. The Army will also be looking for you to be mature for your age and that there are no signs of depression or anxiety. They will also be assessing your ability to cope well with unfamiliar surroundings and that you will not become homesick during training.

Tips for scoring high in emotional maturity and stability:

- During the interviews and during discussions with the Armed Forces Careers Officer advisor, try to provide examples of where you have dealt well with difficult situations in your life in a positive and mature manner;
- Try to be upbeat and positive about the future;
- Don't be overconfident or macho.

DRIVE AND DETERMINATION TO SUCCEED

The Army want to know that you have a sense of purpose in your life. They will be looking for a pattern of achievement, either through school, university or at work, and for evidence that you are not easily deflected from your goals and aspirations. They want to see that you are a competitive person who is highly motivated to succeed. Perseverance is my favourite word. If I persevere, then I will be successful. Drive and determination are very similar to perseverance in that you have the ability to keep working hard and improving yourself until you achieve success.

Those applicants who show signs that they give up easily or have no goals or aspirations will score poorly in the area of drive and determination to succeed.

Tips for scoring high in drive and determination to succeed:

- Provide examples of where you have achieved. This might be educational qualifications, courses that you have attended, or even sporting achievements;
- Be positive about joining the Army and tell them that nothing is going to stop you from succeeding. If you don't pass this time then you will look for ways to improve for the next time you apply;
- Demonstrate that your ambition and sense of purpose is to join the Army and become a professional and competent officer.

PHYSICALLY ROBUST

The Army want to see that you engage in outdoor activities and that you have some experience in playing team sports. Being physically active is important and if you are strong and free from injuries and weakness then this will be an advantage during selection. If you are not involved in any form of team sports then we advise that you start straight away. It is very easy to become involved in team sports, as there are so many to choose from.

Examples of team sports include football, hockey, rugby and basketball.

Those applicants who provide evidence that they are generally isolated individuals who spend too much time at home on the computer or watching TV will score lower than those who are physically active.

Tips for scoring high in physical robustness:

- Be involved in competitive team sports;
- Be an active outdoor type person;
- Attend the gym and carry out light weight exercises and workouts.

EXPERIENCE OF BEING SELF-RELIANT

The Army want to know that you can handle the pressure of living away from home. If you have travelled or have been on camps where you have had to 'rough it' then this would be an advantage. Basically, they want to know that you can look after yourself without the help of your parents or home comforts.

If you have no experience whatsoever of being self-reliant then we advise that you take steps to improve your experience of this area. For example, there is nothing to stop you from going camping for the weekend or joining the Army Cadets where you will be able to gain experience of this important attribute.

Tips for scoring high in being self-reliant

- Provide examples of where you have been away from home for short or long periods of time;
- Tell the interviewer that you enjoy travelling and being away from home. Remember that it is important to provide examples of where you have already done this.
- Tell the interviewer that you are looking forward to leaving home to join the Army and face the challenges that it presents;
- Provide examples of where you have had to fend for yourself or where you have been away camping.

REACTIONS TO SOCIAL DISCIPLINE

The Army want to see that you have a positive attitude towards authority. People in authority include the police, your parents, teachers and even your boss at work. When you join the Army you will initially be taking orders from senior officers and they want to know that you have no problem with authority. As you progress through your career and complete your Officer Initial Training, it will be you who is giving the orders.

There is a strong possibility that the interviewer will ask you questions that relate to your attitude to education and your teachers. At no point should you be negative about your teachers or about people whom are in positions of authority. If you are disrespectful or negative about these people then there is a strong possibility that the Army selection officers will take a dim view on your attitude and you won't be put forward to the AOSB briefing. For example, there have been applicants who complain during the Army Interview that their teachers were rubbish at their job and that everyone in the class would always laugh at them. As you can imagine, those applicants do not progress any further during the selection process.

Tips for scoring high in social discipline:

- Try to provide examples of where you have carried out orders, either at work or at school;
- Tell the interviewer that you respect authority, providing you do of course, and that you see it as an important aspect of life. You do not have a problem with taking orders from anyone, even if they are the opposite sex to you.

EXPERIENCE AND REACTION TO REGIMENT AND ROUTINE

When you join the Army you will initially lose much of your personal freedom. During your initial training there will be many restrictions placed upon you in terms of leave and your general freedom. You won't be given the time to do all of the things that you usually do whilst at home. Therefore, the Army want to see that you have the ability to cope with this added pressure and disciplined routine.

You must try to demonstrate during the selection process that you have already experienced some form of routine and that you are capable of following rules and regulations. This could simply be by having some form of disciplined routine at home, whereby you are required to clean the house and carry out the ironing for a few hours every week.

Tips for scoring high in experience of and reaction to regimentation and routine:

- Provide examples of where you have lost your personal freedom, either during your upbringing, at school or during work. Maybe you have had to work unsociable hours or had to dedicate time and effort into your educational studies or degree course?
- Tell the interviewer that you fully understand that you will lose your personal freedom when you join the Army and that it won't be a problem for you.
- Implement some form of routine into your preparation strategy for joining the Army. Set out your action plan early on and follow it rigidly.

Having knowledge of Army life can be achieved in a number of ways. If you have been a member of any youth organisations then this will be an obvious advantage. Youth organisations include the Scouts, Army Cadets, Air Training Corps or Sea Cadets etc. If members of your family or friends are in the Armed Forces then you can also gain knowledge by asking them questions about their job and life within the Armed Forces. It is also important to gain knowledge of Army life by reading your recruitment literature and visiting the Army website if you have access to the Internet.

Another fantastic way to gain invaluable knowledge of how the Army operates and its equipment is to grab yourself a copy of the book entitled *The British Army: A Pocket Guide*. This book usually sells for approximately £5.99 and it fits easily into your pocket. Any spare moments you have during the day you can get the book out and start reading about vital facts that relate to the British Army.

Tips for scoring high in knowledge and experience of Army life:

- Speak to any friends or relatives who are members of the Armed Forces and ask them what it is like. Gain as much information as possible from the Armed Forces Careers Office staff and also through your recruitment literature;

- Find out as much as possible about the training you will undertake when you join the Army for your chosen career and also your initial recruit training;
- Consider visiting an Army establishment or museum. These are great places to learn about Army life.
- Consider joining a youth organisation such as the Scouts or cadets to gain some experience of a disciplined service.

MOTIVATION FOR JOINING THE ARMY

The Army want to see that it is your own decision to join and that you haven't been pushed into it by friends or your family. They want to see that you have been pulled by the attractions of the Army as opposed to being pushed into them. If you are successful in your application the Army will be investing a tremendous amount of time, energy and finances into your training and development. The last thing they want is that you decide it's not for you.

Tips for scoring high in motivation to join the Army:

- Always present a positive attitude towards joining when you visit the Armed Forces Careers Office and also whilst attending the AOSB. This choice of career should be something that you considered very carefully and have been working very hard to make sure that you pass
- Try to think about what attracts you to the Army and tell the interviewer during selection.

PERSONAL CIRCUMSTANCES

The Army will want to know that you have the support of your family and/or your partner. They also want to see that you are free from any detracting circumstances such as financial difficulties. If you are in financial difficulty, then this could have a negative effect on your mental health during training. They will assess your personal circumstances during selection and also at the AOSB interviews.

Tips for scoring high in personal circumstances:

- Speak to your parents and your partner (if applicable) about your choice of career. Ask them for their support;
- If they do not support you or they are concerned about you joining then we would recommend that you take them along to the careers office so that the Armed Forces Careers Officer can talk to them about Army life and answer any questions that they may have. It is imperative that you have their full support.

EXPERIENCE OF LEADERSHIP AND MANAGEMENT

Because you are applying to join the Army as an Officer, it would be wise to gain some experience as a leader or manager before you apply. The Army will ask you the question "What experience do you have so far as a leader or manager?" If you don't have any experience in these important areas then how do you know you'll make a good Army Officer?

There are many ways in which you can gain supervisory, leadership or managerial experience:

- Ask your manager at work if you can shadow him/her for a week to see how they manage their staff and their responsibilities.
- Take charge of a sporting team.
- Arrange a charity event with a group of friends and volunteer to be the one who organises and arranges the event.
- Volunteer to be the captain of a sporting team.

It is important that you try to gain some form of managerial experience before you join. During the next section of this guide we have provided you with some useful information as to how you will be assessed during the AOSB.

THE AOSB SCORING CRITERIA

Before we go onto explain the scoring criteria, let us first of all take a look at some of the competencies required to successfully pass Army Officer Initial Training at Sandhurst.

COMPETENCIES REQUIRED FOR SUCCESS DURING INITIAL OFFICER TRAINING

Interpersonal Competencies:

Communication – Communicates accurately and effectively, both orally and in writing.

Teamwork – Works willingly with others to achieve common goals.

Influencing – Persuades others to follow a certain course of action.

Problem Solving Competencies

Appreciation – Comprehends, identifies, extracts, and assimilates information from a range of sources, quickly and accurately.

Reasoning – Thinks logically, practically and coherently to produce a successful or reasonable solution, quickly and accurately.

Organisation – Determines priorities and allocates resources effectively and efficiently to a task(s).

Capacity – Holds and processes multiple inputs whilst maintaining task performance.

Character Competencies

Decisiveness – Makes sound appropriate decisions within time-scale demanded by the situation.

Self-motivation – Demonstrates a high level of commitment and interest to tasks.

Self-analysis – Monitors and objectively analyses own performance.

Integrity – Behaviour is guided by principles, morals and ethics appropriate to service life. Adheres to rules and regulations specific to the Army.

Now that we understand some of the competencies that are required to pass Officer Initial Training, we can explore the assessable qualities required in order to successfully pass the Army Officer Main Board.

SOME OF THE COMPETENCIES ASSESSED DURING AOSB MAIN BOARD

Oral & Written Communication – Delivery, effectiveness/understanding, listening. Is able to write in a clear, relevant and concise manner.

Teamwork – Can work with others to achieve a common goal or task, treatment of others, effort and determination.

Influencing – Impact on others; directing, persuasiveness.

Problem Solving – Judgment/reasoning, flexibility, comprehension, capacity, decisiveness.

Confidence and Resilience – Self-assurance, composure, perseverance, assertion.

The Army will use these and other competencies to assess your performance during the AOSB Main Board. It is therefore imperative that you score positively in every area. Each of the competencies are assessed during every stage and it is therefore important that you try to demonstrate them.

CHAPTER 4
THE ARMY CAREERS ADVISOR (ACA) INTERVIEW

During the Army Officer Selection process you will be required to sit interviews at both the Armed Forces Careers Office (AFCO) and also during your attendance at the Army Officer Selection Board (AOSB). Whilst the questions and tips contained within this section of the guide concentrate primarily on the AFCO interview, they are also great preparation for the AOSB too.

The interview, which is held at your local Armed Forces Careers Office, will be undertaken by an Army Careers Advisor. The purpose of this interview is to 'filter' out those people who have the potential to become an Army Officer and those that don't. If you have the potential, then you will get put forward to attend the AOSB briefing.

The duration of the initial AFCO interview will very much depend on your responses to the questions. However, you can expect the interview to last for approximately 60 minutes. The questions that you will be assessed against during the initial interview will normally be taken from the following areas:

→ The reasons why you want to join the Army and why you have chosen this service over the Royal Navy and the Royal Air Force;

→ Why you want to become an Army Officer and what skills, qualities and experiences you have that would help you to become a competent officer.

→ What choice of career you are most interested in, the reason for choosing that career, and the skills you have to match the role;

→ What information you already know about the Army, its history, its lifestyle and training;

→ Information relating to your hobbies and interests including sporting/team activities;

→ Any personal responsibilities that you currently have at home, in your education or at work;

→ Information about your family and your partner and what they think about you joining;

→ Your educational qualifications;

→ Information based around your initial application and CV;

→ Your experience of work and education;

→ Your emotional stability and your maturity;

→ Your drive and determination to succeed;

→ Experiences that you have already gained as a manager, leader or supervisor;

→ Having a positive reaction to a disciplined environment and towards people in positions of authority.

Before moving onto a number of sample interview questions and responses we want to explain a little bit about interview technique and how you can come across in a positive manner during the interview.

During his career in the Fire Service Richard sat on many interview panels assessing people who wanted to become firefighters. As you can imagine there were some good applicants and there were also some poor ones. Richard will explain the difference between a good applicant and a poor one in the section below. Following this Richard, will provide a number of sample interview questions and answers.

A GOOD APPLICANT

A good applicant is someone who has taken the time to prepare. They have researched both the organisation they are applying to join and also the role that they are being interviewed for. They may not know every detail about the organisation and the role but it will be clear that they have made an effort to find out important facts and information. They will be well presented at the interview and they will be confident, but not over confident. As soon as they walk into the interview room they will be polite and courteous and they will sit down in the interview chair only when invited to do so. Throughout the interview they will sit upright in the chair and communicate in a positive manner. If they do not know the answer to a question they will say so and they won't try and waffle. At the end of the interview they will ask positive questions about the job or the organisation before shaking hands and leaving.

A POOR APPLICANT

A poor applicant could be any combination of the following. They will be late for the interview or even forget to turn up at all. They will have made little effort to dress smart and they will have carried out little or no preparation. When asked questions about the job or the organisation they will have little or no knowledge. Throughout the interview they will appear to be unenthusiastic about the whole process and will look as if they want the interview to be over as soon as possible. Whilst sat in the interview chair they will slouch and fidget. At the end of the interview they will try to ask clever questions that are intended to impress the panel. I strongly advise that you try out a 'mock' interview before the real thing. You'll be amazed at how much your confidence will improve. All you need to do is get your parents or a friend to sit down with you and ask you the interview questions that are contained within this guide. Try the answer them as if you were at the real interview. The more mock interviews you try the more confident you'll become.

INTERVIEW TECHNIQUE

How you present yourself during the interview is important. Whilst assessing candidates for interviews I will not only assess their responses to the interview questions but I will also pay attention to the way they present themselves. A candidate could give excellent responses to the interview questions but if they present themselves in a negative manner then this can lose them marks.

Take a look at the following diagrams which indicate both poor technique and good technique.

POOR INTERVIEW TECHNIQUE

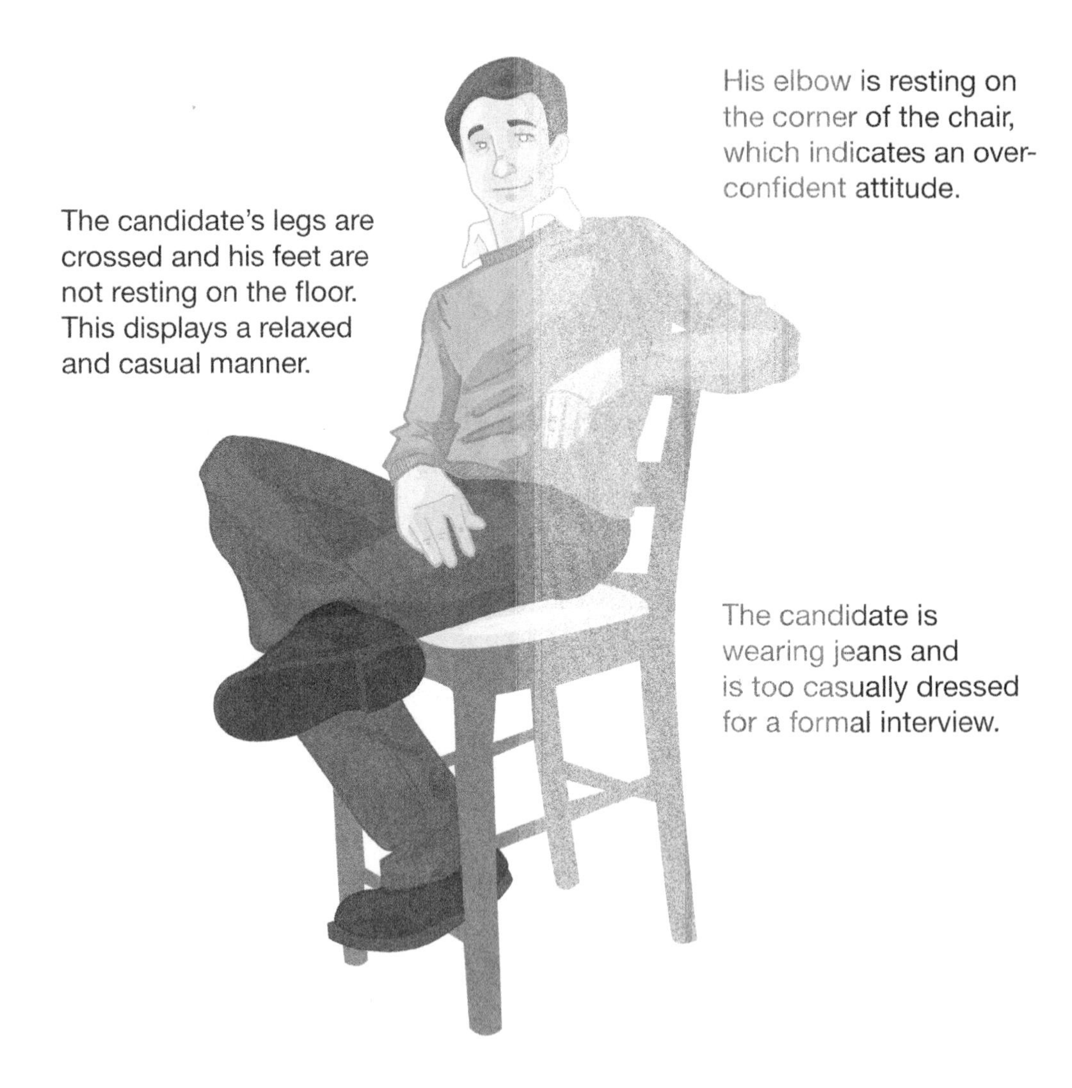

The candidate appears to be too relaxed and casual for an interview.

GOOD INTERVIEW TECHNIQUE

The candidate is smiling and he portrays a confident, but not over-confident manner.

The candidate is dressed wearing a smart suit. It is clear that he has made an effort in his presentation.

His hands are in a stable position, which will prevent him from fidgeting. He could also place his hands palms facing downwards and resting on his knees.

He is sitting upright in the interview chair with his feet resting on the floor. He is not slouching and he portrays himself in a positive manner.

In the build up to your initial ACA interview, practice a few 'mock' interviews. Look to improve your interview technique as well as working on your responses to the interview questions.

Now let's take a look at a number of sample interview questions. Please note that these questions are not guaranteed to be the exact ones you will come up against at the real interview, but they are a great starting point in your preparation. Use the sample responses that I have provided as a basis for your own preparation. Construct your answers on your own opinions and experiences.

THE ARMED FORCES CAREERS OFFICE INTERVIEW

During the Army Officer selection process you will be required to sit a number of interviews both at the AFCO and at the AOSB. The information that I have provided within this section of the guide will assist you during your preparation for both sets of interviews.

The Army will use a set marking sheet for your interviews and the questions will be based around a number of specific criteria. The questions will vary from interview to interview but the core elements are designed to assess whether you are suitable to join the service as an Officer and progress onto the AOSB. The following is a list of areas you may be asked questions on during your Army Careers Advisor interview and I would recommend that you use these as a basis for your preparation:

- The reasons why you want to join the Army.
- The reasons why you want to become an Officer.
- The reasons why you have chosen your particular job, trade and Regiment.
- What information you already know about the Army, your chosen Regiment and the lifestyle and training.
- Information about your hobbies and interests including sporting activities.
- Any personal responsibilities that you currently have at home, at college/ university or at work.
- Information about your family and what they think about you joining the Army. Do they support you?
- Information based around your initial application form.
- Your experience of work and education and whether or not you have had any responsibility at home or work.
- Any positions of authority you have held either at school, college, university, work or otherwise.
- Your emotional stability and your maturity.

- Your drive and determination to succeed.
- Any experience you have of working as part of a team.
- Your attitude towards physical exercise and team sports.
- Having a positive reaction to the disciplined environment.
- Your knowledge of life within the Army.

Over the next few pages I have provided you with a number of sample interview questions and responses. These will act as a good basis for your preparation. However, it is important to point out at this stage the responses you provide during the interview should be based solely on your own experiences and opinions.

SAMPLE INTERVIEW QUESTION NUMBER 1

Why do you want to join the Army?

This is an almost guaranteed question during your ACA interview so there should be no reason why you can't answer it in a positive manner. Try to display motivation when answering questions of this nature. The Army are looking for people who want to become professional members of their team and who understand the Army way of life. By studying your Army recruitment literature and the Army website you will understand what service life is all about. You want to be an Officer of the British Army, and you are attracted to what it has to offer. If you have been pushed into joining by your family then you shouldn't be applying.

SAMPLE RESPONSE TO QUESTION NUMBER 1

'I have wanted to join the Army for a number of years now and feel that I have now reached a part of my life where I am ready to commit to the service. Having studied the Army recruitment literature and visited the Army website, I am impressed by the professionalism and standards the service sets itself.

I would like a career that is fulfilling, challenging and rewarding and I believe that the Army would provide all of these. I enjoy keeping physically fit and active and believe that given the right training I would make a great team member. I am also very much attracted to the fact that the Army offers a wide choice of careers.

The fact that I would be improving my education and receiving highly professional training as an Officer is just another example of why I want to join the service. I have seriously considered the implications that joining the Army would have on both my personal life and social life and discussed these with my family. They have given me their full support and commitment in helping me to achieve my goal of joining the Army as an Officer.'

SAMPLE INTERVIEW QUESTION NUMBER 2

What does your family think of you wanting to join the Army?

Again, you are likely to be asked a question surrounding your family background and what they think about you wanting to join the Army. It is important that your family support you in your decision. If they have any doubts about you joining the service then you may wish to consider taking them along to the AFCO, so they can ask any questions or raise any concerns that they may have. When answering questions such as this, it is important that you are honest and tell the truth. If your family has any concerns, share them with the careers officer, who will then be able to advise you on the best way for your family/partner to overcome any fears they may have.

SAMPLE RESPONSE TO QUESTION NUMBER 2

'I have discussed the issue with them in depth and also shown them all of the Army recruitment literature to try to dampen any fears that they may have. They were initially concerned about me joining but gave me their full support once I told them everything I know about the Officer Initial Training I will receive and the conditions I will serve under. They are aware that the Army has a formidable reputation and this has helped them to further understand why I want to join. They have seen how enthusiastic I am about wanting to join the Army and know that it will be great for me. I have also discussed the issue with my partner and he/she is extremely supportive.'

SAMPLE INTERVIEW QUESTION NUMBER 3

How do you think you will cope with Army life in relation to the discipline and being part of a military organisation?

When you join the Army you will be joining a military organisation that has set procedures, standards and discipline codes. To some people this will come as a shock and the Army wants to know that you are prepared for this change in lifestyle. They are investing time, effort and resources into your training so they want to know that you can cope with their way of life.

When answering this type of question you need to demonstrate both your awareness of what Army life involves and also your positive attitude towards the disciplined environment. Study the recruitment literature and visit the Army website to get a feel for the type of training you will be going through.

SAMPLE RESPONSE TO QUESTION NUMBER 3

'Having read the information available to me about the Army way of life, I think I would cope very well. I know that I will find it difficult at times but believe I have both the maturity and stability to succeed and become a competent and professional officer. The very nature of the Army means that it requires a disciplined workforce. Without discipline things can go wrong. If I am successful and do not carry out my duties professionally then I could endanger somebody's life. I understand why discipline is required and believe I would cope with it well. I understand that being in the Army isn't a 9-5 job, but instead you must take on tasks whenever required.

In order to prepare for the training I have already integrated routine and self-discipline into my life. For example, I have been getting up at 6am every weekday morning to go running and I have started carrying out daily household tasks such as hovering, cleaning and ironing. At the start of my preparation for joining the Army I made myself an action plan that would focus my mind on what I needed to do in order to improve.'

SAMPLE INTERVIEW QUESTION NUMBER 4

How do you think you will cope with being away from home and losing your personal freedom?

This type of question is one that needs to be answered positively. There is only one correct answer to this question and you need to demonstrate that you have considered the consequences of leaving home and are fully aware of what is involved. If you have any experience of being away from home then you should state this in your response. Try to think of occasions when you have been away for periods of time and tell them that it wasn't an issue.

Have you ever been a part of any youth organisations? If you have then this will undoubtedly go in your favour. Giving an example is far better than just saying you will be able to cope.

SAMPLE RESPONSE TO QUESTION NUMBER 4

'Having already had experience of being away from home, I believe I would cope extremely well. Whilst serving with the Scouts a few years ago I was introduced to the Army way of life and fully understand what it is like to be away from home. I actually enjoy being away from home and I can't wait to get started if I am successful during officer selection. I understand, however, that the training is difficult and intense and I am fully prepared for this. I am confident that I will cope with the change in lifestyle very well and I am looking forward to the challenge if I am accepted.'

SAMPLE INTERVIEW QUESTION NUMBER 5

Are you involved in any sporting activities and how do you keep yourself fit?

When answering questions based around your own physical fitness you need to be honest but bear in mind the following points:

Although you don't have to be super fit to join the Army, you do need to have a good level of physical fitness, so being fit in the first instance is an obvious advantage. You will also be acting as a role model to the men and women under your command. You therefore cannot expect them to maintain their levels of fitness, if you cannot maintain your own.

The Army, just like the other Armed Forces, pride themselves on their ability to work as an effective team unit. Those people who engage in active team sports are more likely to be competent team members. If you play a team sport then this will be a good thing to tell them. If you don't then it may be a good idea to go and join one!

Regardless of the above points, remember that if you don't do any physical activity whatsoever then you will score low in this area. Make sure you partake in some form of physical activity. During the AOSB, both briefing and main boards, you will be required to carry out the multi-stage fitness test. Get a copy of the test now from www.How2Become.com and start building it into your preparation.

SAMPLE RESPONSE TO QUESTION NUMBER 5

'Yes I am. I currently play in the local hockey team and have been doing that for a number of years now. Maintaining a good level of fitness is something I enjoy. In fact, recently I have increased my fitness levels by going swimming three times a week. I'm aware that during the Officer Initial Training course I will be pushed to my limits so I need to be prepared for that. I believe the fact that I play team sports will help me get through my training.

I enjoy playing in a hockey team because when we are being beaten by another team everyone always pulls together and we work hard to try to win the game back. After the game we all meet in the club bar for a drink and chat about the game. Keeping fit is important to me and something that I want to continue doing throughout my career if I am successful in joining the Army.'

SAMPLE INTERVIEW QUESTION NUMBER 6

How do you think you will fit into a team environment?

Once again, it would be a positive thing if you can demonstrate you have experience of working in a team. Maybe you have experience of working in a sporting team or need to work as a team in your current job? Try to think of examples where you have already been working in a team environment and if you can provide an example where the team achieved something then even better. Structure your answer around your own experiences and also around your knowledge of the fact that the Army needs to work as an effective team unit in order for it to complete its tasks both safely and on time.

SAMPLE RESPONSE TO QUESTION NUMBER 6

'I have experience of working in a team and I really enjoyed it, so I know I would fit in well. I play for my local rugby team and it is important that everybody gels together in order to win our games. The real test for the team is when we are being beaten and I always try to rally the team together and get us motivated to win back the points we have lost. I understand that the Army needs to work together effectively as a team to get the right result. If the team doesn't perform then people's lives can be put at risk. Being an effective part of the team also means that I would have to train hard and keep up my competency levels, which I believe I would do well.

With my experience of team sports and having the ability to pull a team together when the chips are down, I think I would be a great asset to the Army team.'

SAMPLE INTERVIEW QUESTION NUMBER 7

What do you do in your spare time?

With questions of this nature the Army Careers Advisor is looking to see if you use your leisure time wisely. Your response will tell them a lot about your attitude and motivation. We all know that some people spend their spare time doing nothing, watching TV or spending hours on Facebook. When you join the Army as an Officer you won't have much time to sit around and do nothing. The Army will want to hear that you are active and doing worthwhile things during your spare time. For example, if you are involved in any sports, outdoor activities or are part of any youth organisation such as the Army Cadets, then these are good things to tell them. You may also be involved in voluntary work or charity work and once again these will work in your favour if mentioned at interview.

If you currently do very little with your spare time then now is a good time to make a lifestyle change. Embark on a fitness routine or join an activity club or organisation.

SAMPLE RESPONSE TO QUESTION NUMBER 7

'During my spare time I like to keep active, both physically and mentally. I enjoy visiting the gym three times a week and I have a structured workout that I try to vary every three months to keep my interest levels up. I'm also currently doing a part-time study course in Art, which is one of my hobbies. I'm also a member of the local Army Cadets, which is an evening's commitment every week and the occasional weekend.

Of course, I know when it is time to relax and usually do this by either listening to music or playing snooker with my friends, but overall I'm quite an active person. I certainly don't like sitting around doing nothing. I understand that if I'm successful at joining the Army there will be plenty of things to do in the evenings to keep me occupied such as the gym, study time and various social events.'

SAMPLE INTERVIEW QUESTION NUMBER 8

Can you tell us about any personal achievements you have experienced during your life so far?

Having achieved something in your life demonstrates that you have the ability to see things through to the end. It also shows that you are motivated and determined to succeed. This is especially true when applying to become an Army Officer. The Army wants to see evidence that you can achieve, as there is a greater chance of you completing the Officer Initial Training course at Sandhurst if you have a history of this. Try to think of examples where you have succeeded or achieved something relevant in your life. Some good examples of achievements are as follows:

- Duke of Edinburgh Award;
- A-levels, degrees or educational qualifications;
- Team or individual sports awards/trophies/medals;
- Raising money for charity.

Obviously you will have your own achievements that you will want to add in your response.

SAMPLE RESPONSE TO QUESTION NUMBER 8

'So far in my life I have managed to achieve a number of things that I am proud of. To begin with, I recently worked hard to achieve my 'A' level results, which enabled me to go on to university to study for my degree. Without these grades I would not have been able to do that. About a year ago the football team that I play in won the league trophy for the second year running, which is another one of my more recent achievements. I was particularly pleased because I was the Captain of the team and played a large part in its organisation and development.

However, my most memorable achievement to date is managing to raise £4,000 for a local charity. I worked hard and ran a marathon in order to raise the money. I was particularly proud of this achievement because It meant the charity I ran for were able to purchase some important items of equipment that could be used to treat some of their patients.'

SAMPLE INTERVIEW QUESTION NUMBER 9

What are your strengths?

This is a common interview question, which is relatively easy to answer. The problem with it is that many people use the same response. It is quite an easy thing to tell the interviewer that you are dedicated and the right person for the job. However, it is a different thing backing it up with evidence!

If you are asked this type of question make sure you are positive during your response and show that you actually mean what you are saying. Then, back your answer up with examples of when you have demonstrated a strength that you say you have. For example, if you tell the panel that you are a motivated person, then back it up with an event in your life where you achieved something through sheer motivation and determination.

SAMPLE RESPONSE TO QUESTION NUMBER 9

'To begin with I am a determined person who likes to see things through to the end. For example, I recently ran a marathon for charity. I'd never done this kind of thing before and found it very hard work, but I made sure I completed the task. Another strength of mine is that I'm always looking for ways to improve myself. As an example, whilst preparing for Officer selection I have embarked on a Diploma in Management Studies through the Open University to give me an insight into management and leadership.

Finally, I would say that one of my biggest strengths is that I'm a great team player. I really enjoy working in a team environment and achieving things through a collaborative approach. For example, I play in a local rugby team and we recently won the league trophy for the first time since the club was established some 50 years ago.'

SAMPLE INTERVIEW QUESTION NUMBER 10

What is your biggest weakness?

Now there's a question! If we were all totally honest with ourselves we could probably write a whole list of weaknesses. Now I wouldn't advise that you reel off a whole list of weaknesses in your interview as you could do yourself a lot of harm. Conversely, those people who say that they don't have any weaknesses are probably not telling the truth.

If you are asked a question of this nature then it is important that you give at least one weakness. The trick here is to make the weakness sound like a strength. For example, a person may say that one of their weaknesses is that their own personal standards are too high sometimes and they expect this of others. Or another one is that a person doesn't know when to relax. They are always on the go achieving and making things happen when they should take more time out to relax and recuperate.

SAMPLE RESPONSE TO QUESTION NUMBER 10

'That's a difficult question but I know that I do have a particular weakness. The standards that I always set myself are quite high and unfortunately, I get frustrated when other people's standards don't match my own. For example, I am hardly ever late for anything and believe that punctuality is really important. However, if I'm left waiting for other people who are late I usually have to say something to them when they finally arrive, which isn't always a good thing.'

SAMPLE INTERVIEW QUESTION NUMBER 11

Can you tell me why you want to become an Officer?

Once again, an almost guaranteed question so make sure you have prepared for it fully. You must have valid reasons why you want to become an Officer in the Army. This job is entirely different to being a regular soldier. You will have far more responsibilities and the training that you will undergo will be extremely challenging, both mentally and physically. Here are a few positive reasons for wanting to become an Officer:

"An opportunity to become an elite Officer in the Army is an opportunity to be the best that I can be."

"I believe that I have the potential to become an exceptional Officer and I don't want to waste my potential."

"I want to become an Officer simply because I believe I have the skills and attributes to lead, inspire and develop people. If I am not in a leadership position then I believe those skills and attributes will be wasted."

"I am a confident, professional and enthusiastic person who believes that everyone should be given the opportunity to be their best. As an Officer I would have the chance to make a difference and I would thrive in a position that could help the Army to achieve its organizational goals and objectives."

"In any organisation that I have worked in so far, I have always held a keen interest in the development of staff and the development of the company as a whole. The experiences that I have gained in life so far have prepared me to become an Officer in the Army and I believe that I could be an excellent member of the Army's leadership team."

SAMPLE INTERVIEW QUESTION NUMBER 12

What qualities do you think you need to be a good team player?

The Army needs effective and competent team players. If you already have some experience of working in a team environment then this will work in your favour. Try to think of examples where you have already successfully contributed to a team task either at work or during your education. There are many different qualities required to work as an effective team player. Here are just a few:

- Enthusiastic;
- A good communicator;
- Motivated;
- Supportive of the other team members;
- Providing other team members with encouragement;
- Determined to complete the task;
- Professional and competent;
- Always focused on the wider team objective.

Now take a look at the following sample response to this question.

SAMPLE RESPONSE TO INTERVIEW QUESTION NUMBER 12

'First of all I believe a team player must be focused purely on the task that the team is trying to achieve. You must always be professional and supportive of the other team members. For example, if one of the team members is struggling then you should try to help them and support them with their role within the team. It is important as a team player to listen to the brief or details of the task and to communicate properly with everyone else in the team. You must always put the needs of the team before your own and be totally committed to completing the task in hand. In relation to being an Officer then it is your responsibility to lead, motivate and lead your team towards the goals and missions of the Army.'

SAMPLE INTERVIEW QUESTION NUMBER 13

What contact have you had with the Army during your application and what have you done to find out about Army life?

Those applicants who are serious about a career in the Army will have gone out of their way to find out about the service and what it involves. The Army Careers Advisor will want to see evidence that you have taken steps to speak to people who are already serving and that you have researched the organisation effectively. It is important that you are 100% committed to joining and that you are fully aware of the challenge that lies ahead of you. The following is a sample response to this question.

SAMPLE RESPONSE TO INTERVIEW QUESTION NUMBER 13

'During my preparation I have carried out lots of research into the Army so that I am fully aware of the challenge that lies ahead of me. To begin with I have studied my recruitment literature in depth and I have also spent plenty of time browsing the Army recruitment website. I have also obtained a copy of the British Army Pocket Guide which has taught me lots about the service, the regiments and the equipment. More recently I spent a couple of hours at my local Army establishment where I managed to speak to serving officers about their role and the job. I found this an invaluable insight. All of this research and reading has made me more excited about joining. I cannot wait to get started if I am successful.'

SAMPLE INTERVIEW QUESTION NUMBER 14

What are the values of the British Army?

Every soldier and officer is expected to abide by a set of values. Therefore, it is not unreasonable for the Army to expect you to know them when you apply. You are likely to be asked a question that relates to the values during the ACA interview so make sure you know them and what each one of them means. Here is a sample response to this question.

SAMPLE INTERVIEW QUESTION NUMBER 14

'The values of the British Army are selfless commitment, courage, discipline, integrity, loyalty and respect for others. It is important to be strong and aggressive in battle but to also behave properly and demonstrate self-control at all times. Being courageous means facing up to danger and doing what is right at all times. Discipline means having the ability to maintain constant high standards, so that others can rely on you. Integrity means earning the respect and trust of your work colleagues. Loyalty is being faithful to your work colleagues and to your duty and having respect for others mean treating everybody with respect and dignity at all times.'

SAMPLE INTERVIEW QUESTION NUMBER 15

What are you currently doing in order to prepare for your training?

Whilst this question should be generally easy to answer, it does end up throwing many applicants. Most people who apply to join the Army will do little or no preparation for Officer Initial Training until they have received confirmation that they have passed the AOSB. However, if you can show the Army Careers Advisor that you are already preparing for training then this will impress them. Here is a sample response to assist you.

SAMPLE RESPONSE TO INTERVIEW QUESTION NUMBER 15

'Although I haven't yet passed the AOSB I have been preparing thoroughly for my training. To begin with I have created a timetable of preparation which makes sure I work on my weak areas and my overall fitness. Every weekday I am up at 6am and I embark on a 4 mile run. This is so that I can get used to the early starts and so that I can improve my fitness levels. Half way round my run I always make sure I stop and carry out 50 press ups and 50 sit ups. When I get home from work I then sit down for an hour and work on my knowledge of the Army and the branch that I am applying for. Every other day I work on my aptitude test ability and I make sure I read a good quality newspaper so that I am up to date with Army operations and the more important current affairs issues. Finally, I have been working on my household skills such as ironing and cleaning.'

SAMPLE INTERVIEW QUESTION NUMBER 16

Can you tell me what Officer Initial Training consists of?

Before you attend your interview you must find out details about the Army Officer initial training at Sandhurst. This information is available through the Army website at www.army.mod.uk.

FURTHER ACA INTERVIEW QUESTIONS TO PREPARE FOR

- What do you think about your educational exam results? Were they what you expected?
- Where is the Army operating in the World right now?
- What parts of Officer Initial Training do you expect to find the hardest?
- What are you currently doing to improve on your weak areas?
- What is your 1st choice Regiment and why?
- Tell me about your 1st choice Regiment. What do they do and where are they operating right now?
- What are the qualities of an Army Officer?
- What is the role of an Army Officer?

INTERVIEW TIPS FOR THE ACA INTERVIEW

→ When you walk into the interview room stand up straight with your shoulders back. Project an image of confidence;

→ Don't sit down in the interview chair until invited to do so;

→ Sit with your hands resting on your knees, palms downwards. It is OK to use your hands expressively but don't overdo it;

→ Don't slouch in the chair;

→ Speak up and be positive;

→ Smile, be happy and have a sense of humour;

→ Dress as smart as you can and take pride in your appearance. If you don't have a suit make sure you wear a shirt and tie at the very least.

→ Improve your personal administration. By this I mean your personal hygiene and cleanliness. Make sure you have washed and your hands and nails are clean.

→ Make sure you have researched both Army life and your chosen career/careers. This is very important.

→ During the interview do not be negative or disrespectful towards your teachers, parents or people in positions of authority. Remember that you are applying to join a disciplined service.

→ Go the extra mile and learn a little bit about the Army's history if you get time. When the panel asks you 'What can you tell us about the Army?' you will be able to demonstrate that you have made an effort to look into their history as well as their modern-day activities;

→ Be respectful and courteous towards the interview panel. At the end of your response to each question finish off with either 'Sir' or 'Ma'am' or as otherwise instructed.

→ Ask positive questions at the end of the interview. Try not to ask questions such as "How much leave will I get?" or "How often do I get paid?"

→ If you are unsure about a question don't waffle. If you do not know the answer then it is OK to say so. Move on to the next question and put it behind you.

→ Finally, believe in yourself and be confident. A positive attitude will bring positive results!

CHAPTER 5
THE COMMAND TASKS AND OBSTACLE COURSE

During the Army Officer Selection Board you will be required to undertake both an outdoor Leaderless task and a Command task. Both tasks involve the solution of a 'practical' problem over an 'obstacle course'. In the Leaderless task there is no appointed leader, whereas in the Command task each candidate takes their turn as leader and must direct the rest of the group.

Let's now take a look at how you can achieve higher marks in each of the tasks.

THE OUTDOOR LEADERLESS TASK

As the name suggests, this task is performed without a designated leader. The purpose of the assessment is to see how effective you are at working as part of a team and also to identify those people who have leadership potential. Those people who do have leadership potential will naturally come to the front and move the completion of the task forward.

As part of your group you will be provided with a task that must be completed within a set time. The task might be a requirement for your group to move an object from point A to B, with certain restrictions in place, such as avoiding an area of floor space or only using specific items of equipment. Whatever the task/brief, it is important that you work effectively as a member of the team and try to come up with solutions to the problem.

Upon completion of the leaderless tasks, as a team you will compete against other groups, in another leaderless task known as 'The Opening Race'

On the morning of the final day, you will also compete against the other groups, in 'The Final Race'. You should give this leaderless task your maximum effort, this being your final opportunity to show the assessing board your Officer potential.

Before we provide you with a number of tips to help you score higher during the leaderless task, let's take a look at a number of key areas that are essential to the smooth running of any task.

Component 1 – Time

It is important that any team working towards a common goal is aware of the time constraints. Make sure everyone is aware of the time, and keep checking it regularly if the facility exists.

Component 2 – Plan

Every team that is working towards a common goal should have a plan in place. If you don't have a plan, how are you going to achieve the task in hand? The way to compile a successful plan is to ask the team if they have any ideas on how the task could be achieved.

Component 3 – Communication

This is probably the most important component of any team task. Communication means talking to, and listening to, the other members of the team. Get this part wrong and the task is guaranteed to fail.

Component 4 – Allocation of tasks

Everybody in the team will have different 'strengths'. You should try to find out who is good at what, and then allocate tasks accordingly.

Component 5 – Support

It is the duty of every team member to support the other members of the team.

Component 6 – URGENCY!

Regardless of how long you have to complete the task, urgency is a must.

Now let's take a look at a number of tips that will help you to pass the leaderless task.

TIP 1: Although you should not 'take over' the task, you should at every opportunity attempt to demonstrate leadership 'potential'. This can be achieved in a number of ways. Once the brief has been provided, be the first to speak out:

"OK everyone, shall we all form a plan in order to achieve the task in the most effective way possible? Does anyone have any suggestions as to how we can tackle this?"

TIP 2: We recommend that you use the words 'plan' and 'time' during the leaderless task and the command task. These two components are the cornerstone of effective teamwork.

TIP 3: Be supportive of other team members and shout words of encouragement:

"This is great teamwork everyone, keep going!"

TIP 4: If the facility exists, keep an eye on the time.

Tip 5: Suggest allocating tasks to people who have skills in certain areas. For example, if there are any knots that need to be tied, ask if there's anyone in the team who is competent in this area.

TIP 6: Keep going, even if things start to go wrong and time is running out. Remember to always act with a sense of urgency!

TIP 7: Be active and get involved.

THE OUTDOOR COMMAND TASK

The command task is different to the leaderless task in the fact that everyone in the group is required to take charge of an exercise/task.

You will be provided with a brief and you will then have a short period of time to brief the rest of your team and complete the required task. As you can imagine, the command task is harder than the leaderless task, simply because the spotlight is on you. It is crucial that you listen to the brief that will be provided by the boarding officer. Once you have the brief, you will then need to explain your plan to the rest of the group, allocate tasks and generally co-ordinate proceedings.

Briefing the team

Once you have received the brief from the boarding officer you will have a short period of time to come up with a plan in order to achieve the task. Here is an excellent format to follow when briefing any team in a command situation:

S.M.E.A.C.

SITUATION – explain what the situation is.

"OK, gather round team and pay attention whilst I explain the situation. Our task today is to..."

MISSION – once you have explained the situation, tell the team what the mission is.

"Our mission is to..."

EXECUTION – tell your team how you are going to achieve the task including the allocation of tasks (plan).

"We will achieve the task by carrying out XYZ."

ASK QUESTIONS – ask your team if anyone has any questions.

"Is the brief clear team? Does anyone have any questions?"

CHECK FOR UNDERSTANDING – check to see that your team fully understands what is expected from them.

"Is everyone clear of the team task and their role within the team?"

Richard used SMEAC many times in the past during training exercises and also during firefighting operations. It provides a degree of organisation to any team and we recommend that you learn it and use it during the command task when you are the person in charge.

Here's a list of tips to help you score higher during the command task exercise.

TIP 1: When you are not the person in charge, be an effective team leader. Help out as much as possible and get stuck in! You may also wish to shout words of encouragement to the other members of the team.

"Let's keep going everyone, we're doing a great job here."

TIP 2: When you are the allocated person in charge, take control of your team.

"OK everyone, gather around and pay attention to the following brief..."

TIP 3: Be supportive of your team members and get involved when necessary.

TIP 4: When briefing the team, consider using SMEAC.

TIP 5: If things start to go wrong, do not panic. Remain calm and in control. Keep going until the end and try your absolute hardest to complete the task. At the end of the task, whether it has been successful or not, thank your team for their efforts.

TIP 6: Keep an eye on safety. You are the person in charge and therefore responsible for safety.

INDIVIDUAL OBSTACLE COURSE

The final task on the morning of day 3 is the Individual Obstacle Course. Your task is to complete as many circuits of the course within the allowed 3 minutes. The obstacles included in the course can consist of the following:

- A high wall
- 2 × hurdles
- Long jump
- Rope swing
- Walking up steps carrying an object (a painted log)

The best way to prepare for this obstacle course, is to maintain a good all round level of fitness, if this is the case you should be able to complete the obstacle course without major problems. If possible try to mimic the individual elements of the obstacle course, in a safe environment of course!

You could even if desired attend a privately-run obstacle course, this will certainly help to prepare you for the obstacles you will face at the Main Board, it will also help to maintain and improve your overall fitness. If you perform an internet search for 'Obstacle Courses' you will find there are many available, throughout the UK.

CHAPTER 6
PREPARING FOR THE PLANNING EXERCISE

PLANNING EXERCISE

You will most probably find this element of the AOSB the toughest. Before we look at how you can prepare effectively, here's an explanation as to what is involved.

INDIVIDUAL STUDY TIME

Each person will be provided with a copy of the brief/setting. You will then have one hour to sit in silence, read the scenario and come up with a solution to the problem. It is important that you read everything carefully. Do not miss out any of the scenario, as this could hinder you during the group discussion phase and questioning by the assessors. If you miss out anything, the assessors will pick up on it.

GROUP DISCUSSION

Once the hour is complete you will then have a period of time to discuss the scenario, and how you intend to approach it, with the other candidates in your group. During this stage make sure you are vocal and active in the construction of the agreed plan – this is VERY important. Do not be afraid to make suggestions and if you have the confidence in your own plan, try and influence the other members of the group. Pay attention at all times, be involved, and never dismiss someone's suggestions directly out of hand.

It is crucial that you are competent in the use of Speed, Distance and Time (SDT) before you attend the AOSB. Our advice is simple:

> Practice SDT questions every day in the build up to the AOSB. You can obtain free SDT questions at the website: ArmyOfficerSelectionBoard.co.uk.

> You should also practice SDT questions by having someone fire questions at you. This is a lot harder than working them out with a pen and paper!

Finally, be competent in the use of the 24-hour clock. The assessing officers will expect you to use it when answering their questions.

TOP TIPS FOR SCORING HIGH DURING THE PLANNING EXERCISE

- Demonstrate strength of character.
- Don't give in, even if things are going wrong.
- Support your decision and consider all eventualities.
- Improve general arithmetic and be competent in the use of speed, distance and time.
- Be able to calculate SDT questions in your head, as well as being able to write them down. You can practice by getting a member of your family to ask you a series of SDT questions. This is great practice, as you will be under pressure to answer the questions without the use of a calculator or pen and paper.

- Keep an eye on the time. You need to come up with a solution to the problem.
- Be alert and quick to respond to questions.
- Never lie when answering questions from the assessors, they will see straight through it. If you do not know the answer to a question, then just say so.
- Always remain calm. The questioning at the end of the exercise is designed to be tough and assess how well you cope under pressure.

SPEED, DISTANCE AND TIME

Accuracy and agility in speed, distance and time calculations will help you perform well during the Army Officer selection process. The following information will assist you in understanding how to tackle these types of question.

When trying to solve these problems it is important to consider three variables: speed, distance and time. Try not to get too worried as two of these variables will always be known. The easiest way to solve these equations is to use the following formulas:

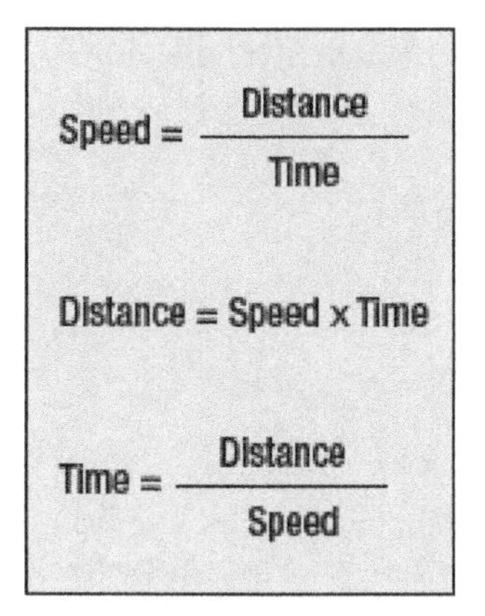

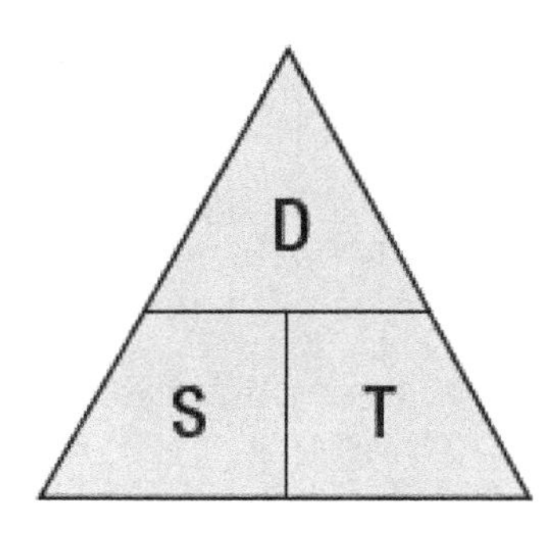

The triangular diagram above is ideal for helping you to remember the formula. Simply place your finger over the variable you are trying to discover, and you will then see the equation required. For example, if you wanted to obtain the time, placing your finger on 'T' would show that you would need to divide distance (D) by speed (S).

Let's now work through some examples:

1. A train travels 60 miles in 3 hours. What is the train's speed?

Formula: Speed = distance ÷ time

Speed = 60 ÷ 3 = 20 mph

2. A car is travelling at 30 mph for 70 minutes. What is the distance travelled? With this problem it is important to remember to work in minutes!

So, 30 mph = 0.5 miles per minute (30 ÷ 60)

70 (minutes) × 0.5 = 35 miles

You can use the formula but you need to convert the minutes into hours and remember that 0.1 = 1/10 of 60 minutes:

Formula: Distance = speed × time

Distance = 30 × 1.1666r (1 hour 10 mins) = 35

3. A tank is driving at 48 mph over 60 miles. How long was it driving for?

Formula: Time = distance ÷ speed

Time = 60 ÷ 48 = 1 hour 15 minutes

Take these steps:

I. You know that 48 mph = 48 miles in 60 minutes.

II. The difference between 60 and 48 is 12, which is ¼ of 48.

III. You can then take ¼ of 60, which gives 15 minutes, and add that to 60 minutes = 75 minutes.

IV. Then convert to hours = 1 hour 15 minutes for the answer! OR

Take these steps:

I. You know that 48 mph = 0.8 miles per minute. II. 60 ÷ 0.8 = 75 minutes.

III. Convert into hours = 1 hour 15 minutes.

Once you understand how to calculate speed, distance and time, take your time to work through the 30 sample test questions that follow.

In order to obtain further Speed, Distance and Time questions, and also try 8 planning exercises, please go to: ArmyOfficerAOSB.co.uk

SAMPLE SPEED, DISTANCE AND TIME TEST QUESTIONS

(Give all distances and speeds in whole numbers)

Question 1

You are travelling at 28mph for 75 minutes. How far do you travel?

Question 2

You travel 15 miles in half an hour. What speed are you travelling at?

Question 3

You travel 33 miles at a constant speed of 55mph. How long are you travelling for?

Question 4

You are travelling at 75 mph for 1 and half hours. How far do you travel?

Question 5

You travel 61 miles in 1 hour and 5 minutes. What speed are you travelling at?

Question 6

You travel 90 miles at a constant speed of 30 mph. How long are you travelling for?

Question 7

You are travelling at 70mph for 126 minutes. How far do you travel?

Question 8

You travel 2.5 miles in 5 minutes. What speed are you travelling at?

Question 9

You travel 75 miles at a constant speed of 45mph. How long are you travelling for?

Question 10

You are travelling at 60 mph for quarter of an hour. How far do you travel?

Question 11

You travel 325 miles in 4 hours and 6 minutes. What speed are you travelling at?

Question 12

You travel 39 miles at 45 mph. How long are you travelling for?

Question 13

You are travelling at 80 mph for 15 minutes. How far do you travel?

Question 14

You travel 63 miles in 54 minutes. What speed are you travelling at?

Question 15

You travel 20 miles at 50 mph. How long are you travelling for?

Question 16

You are travelling at 65 mph for one hour and 12 minutes. How far do you travel?

Question 17

You travel 120 miles in two hours. What speed are you travelling at?

Question 18

You travel 80 miles at 50 mph. How long are you travelling for?

Question 19

You are travelling at 40 mph for half an hour. How far do you travel?

Question 20

You travel 80 miles in 1 hour and 40 minutes. What speed are you travelling at?

Question 21

You travel 35 miles at 70 mph. How long are you travelling for?

Question 22

You are travelling at 15 mph for 8 minutes. How far do you travel?

Question 23

You travel 16 miles in quarter of an hour. What speed are you travelling at?

Question 24

You travel 60 miles at 50 mph. How long are you travelling for?

Question 25

You are travelling at 30 mph for 10 minutes. How far do you travel?

Question 26

You travel 75 miles in one and half hours. What speed are you travelling at?

Question 27

You travel 1 mile at 60 mph. How long are you travelling for?

Question 28

You are travelling at 50 mph for 2 and half hours. How far do you travel?

Question 29

You travel 100 miles in 1 hour and 20 minutes. What speed are you travelling at?

Question 30

You travel 600 miles at 80 mph. How long are you travelling for?

ANSWERS TO SPEED, DISTANCE AND TIME TEST

1. 35 miles
2. 30 mph
3. 36 mins
4. 112.5 miles
5. 56 mph
6. 3 hours
7. 147 miles
8. 30 mph
9. 1hour 40 minutes
10. 15 miles
11. 79 mph
12. 52 mins
13. 20 miles
14. 70 mph
15. 24 mins
16. 78 miles
17. 60 mph
18. 1 hour 36 mins
19. 20 miles
20. 48 mph
21. 30 mins
22. 2 miles
23. 64mph
24. 1 hour 12 mins
25. 5 miles
26. 50 mph
27. 1 minute
28. 125 miles
29. 75 mph
30. 7 hours 30 minutes

On the following pages we have provided you with two sample planning exercises for you to try. Give them a go and see how you get on. There is no time limit for these sample exercises.

PLANNING EXERCISE - SEASIDE MISSION

You are the duty officer in charge at the Royal National Lifeboat Institution's (RNLI) rescue centre at FLITTERBY. The FLITTERBY lifeboat is currently involved in rescuing some sailors from a drifting yacht in the Irish Sea.

It is exactly 10:00 am and the coxswain of the lifeboat has just radioed the following message to you:

"One of the sailors we have taken off from the sinking yacht is desperately ill and must have a blood transfusion as soon as possible. I have just been talking, by radio, to the Accident & Emergency (A&E) staff at ASHBY hospital and they will be standing-by to receive him but have pointed out that every minute counts. Make sure the RNLI's ambulance (a specially adapted estate car) is ready to take him to the hospital as soon as we arrive at the jetty. I cannot give you an exact time of arrival, but it will not be before 10:20 hours, or later than 10:45 hours. Once we are tied up, it will take us 5 minutes to get him from the boat into the ambulance. It will be up to you to get him from the jetty to the A&E dept with the utmost urgency."

You study the map and recollect that there are 3 ways to get to hospital, each with advantages and disadvantages:

1. The route via the gate bridge is subject to delays as the crossings are controlled and the bridge is only open 3 times per hour for 12 minutes. The bridge is open at 10 minutes past, 30 minutes past and 10 minutes to the hour. The journey across the gate bridge will take you 10 minutes. The B120 is twisty and a maximum average speed could be no greater than 40 mph.

2. The route through the centre of ASHBY on the A424 is further but although it should be possible to average 40 mph out of town, once inside the central congestion zone, heavy traffic and narrow streets means no more than 5 mph can be averaged for the 10 miles through the walled part of the town. The one limitation from using the A424 is that from 11:00 hrs onwards the central congestion zone is very dense and traffic is at a standstill.

3. The new A11 by-pass is dual carriage and passes the hospital but, although the longest route, will allow averages of 70 mph to be achieved. It is possible to reach the A11 from FLITTERBY in 10 mins.

You warn the duty driver to stand-by. Unfortunately, you cannot alert the local police on the telephone to make any special arrangements, so there is no way of interrupting the steady but reliable timetable of the gate bridge. The duty officer at nearby RAF Valley tells you the Search and Rescue helicopter is unavailable as it is on a mission rescuing someone from an oil rig miles out to sea.

Your aim is to transport the sailor to the hospital in the quickest time possible.

Question 1

What is the earliest time that the sailor will arrive at RNLI Flitterby?

Question 2

What is the latest time the sailor will arrive at RNLI Flitterby?

Question 3

How long in minutes will it take you to get from RNLI Flitterby to the A11 junction?

Question 4

Based on the sailor arriving at RNLI Flitterby at the latest time possible, which route do you choose and why?

Question 5

Based on the sailor arriving at RNLI Flitterby at the earliest time possible, which route do you choose and why?

NOTE - You are to calculate the total journey times for each of the 3 different routes using Speed, Distance and Time calculations.

YOUR CALCULATIONS

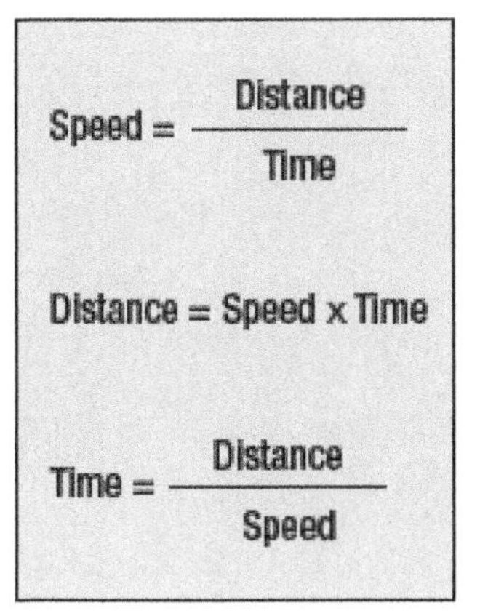

$$\text{Speed} = \frac{\text{Distance}}{\text{Time}}$$

$$\text{Distance} = \text{Speed} \times \text{Time}$$

$$\text{Time} = \frac{\text{Distance}}{\text{Speed}}$$

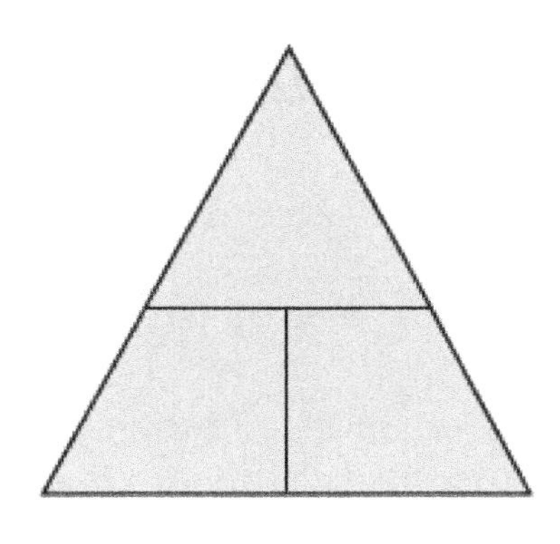

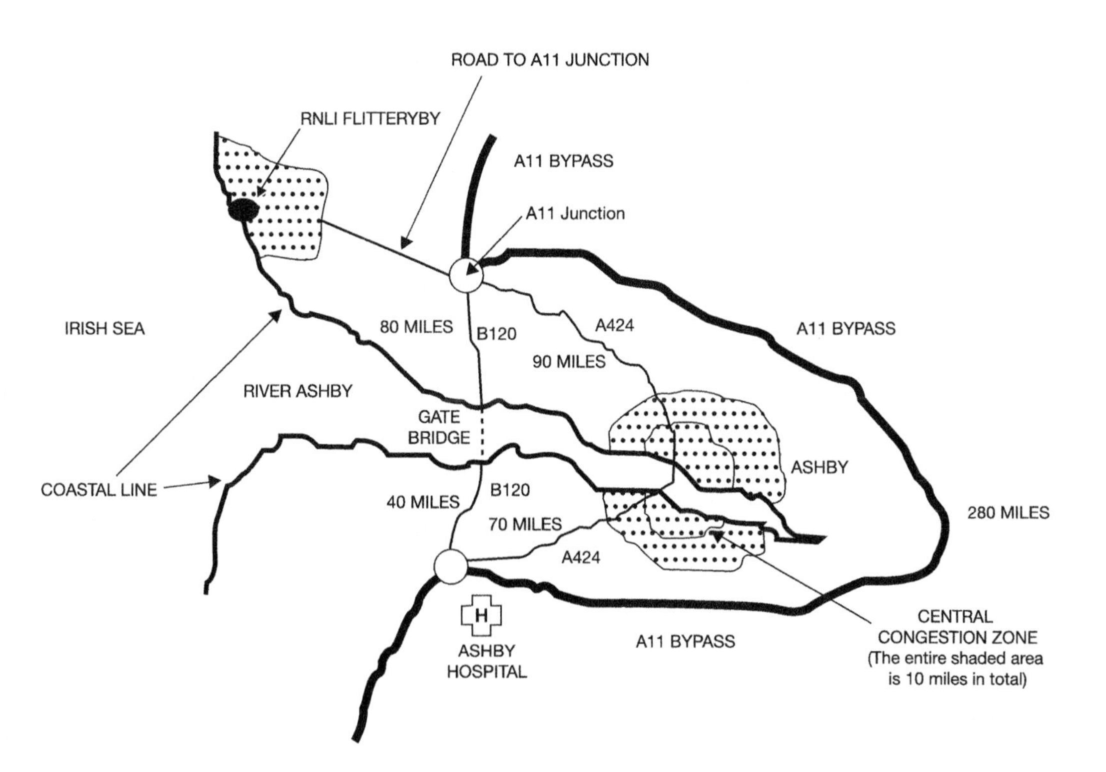

ANSWERS TO QUESTIONS

Question 1

How long in minutes will it take you to get from RNLI Flitterby to the A11 junction?

ANSWER: 10 minutes

Question 2

Based on the sailor arriving at Flitterby at the earliest time possible, what time will you reach the Hospital if you choose route 1?

The sailor arrives at Flitterby at 10:20hrs. It takes 5 minutes to load him into the ambulance which brings the time to 10:25hrs. It takes 10 minutes to get to the A11 junction which brings the time to 10:35hrs.

Travelling route 1, it is a total of 80 miles to the Gate Bridge. We are able to travel at a maximum speed of 40mph. To find out the time it takes to travel this distance we need to use the following calculation:

Time = Distance / Speed

Time = 80 / 40

Answer: 2 hours

We now know that we will arrive at the Gate Bridge at 12:35hrs. From the information provided we know that the Gate Bridge is open 3 times per hour for 12 minutes. The bridge is open at 10 minutes past, 30 minutes past and 10 minutes to the hour.

The bridge is already open when we arrive at 12:35 hours; therefore we are able to cross straight away. The journey across the gate bridge takes us 10 minutes, which means that we will arrive on the other side at 12:45hrs.

We now have to make the final journey along the B120 towards the hospital. The distance is 40 miles in total and we can travel at a maximum speed of 40 miles per hour. In order to calculate the time we need to use the following calculation:

Time = Distance / Speed

Time = 40 / 40

Answer = 1 hour

ANSWER: Arrive at the hospital at 13:45hrs.

Question 3

Based on the sailor arriving at Flitterby at the latest time possible, what time will you reach the Hospital if you choose route 3?

The sailor arrives at Flitterby at 10:45hrs. It takes 5 minutes to load him into the ambulance which brings the time to 10:50hrs. It takes 10 minutes to get to the A11 junction which brings the time to 11:00hrs.

Travelling along route 3 we know that we can achieve a maximum speed of 70 miles per hour. In order to work out the total time it will take us to reach the hospital we need to use the following calculation:

Time = Distance / Speed

Time = 280 / 70

Answer = 4 hours

ANSWER: Arrive at the hospital will be 15:00hrs.

Question 4

Based on the sailor arriving at Flitterby at the latest time possible, what time will you reach the Hospital if you choose route 1?

The sailor arrives at Flitterby at 10:45hrs. It takes 5 minutes to load him into the ambulance which brings the time to 10:50hrs. It takes 10 minutes to get to the A11 junction which brings the time to 11:00hrs.

Travelling route 1, it is a total of 80 miles to the Gate Bridge. We are able to travel at a maximum speed of 40mph. To find out the time it takes to travel this distance we need to use the following calculation:

Time = Distance / Speed

Time = 80 / 40

Answer = 2 hours

We now know that we will arrive at the Gate Bridge at 13:00hrs. From the information provided we know that the Gate Bridge is open 3 times per hour for 12 minutes. The bridge is open at 10 minutes past, 30 minutes past and 10 minutes to the hour.

The bridge is still open when we arrive at 13:00 hours; therefore we are able to cross straight away. The journey across the gate bridge takes us 10 minutes, which means that we will arrive on the other side at 13:10hrs.

We now have to make the final journey along the B120 towards the hospital.

The distance is 40 miles in total and we can travel at a maximum speed of 40 miles per hour. In order to calculate the time we need to use the following calculation:

Time = Distance / Speed

Time = 40 / 40

Answer = 1 hour

ANSWER: Arrive at the hospital at 14:10hrs.

Question 5

Based on the sailor arriving at Flitterby at the earliest time possible, what time will you reach the Hospital if you choose route 2?

The sailor arrives at Flitterby at 10:20hrs. It takes 5 minutes to load him into the ambulance which brings the time to 10:25hrs. It takes 10 minutes to get to the A11 junction which brings the time to 10:35hrs.

We know that the distance from the A11 junction to the edge of the congestion zone is a total of 90 miles. We also know that the distance from the other side of the congestion zone to the hospital along the A424 is a total of 70 miles. Therefore we can add these two distances together to get a total distance (minus the congestion zone area) of 160 miles. In order to work out the time it takes to travel this distance we need to use the following calculation:

Time = Distance / Speed

Time = 160 / 40

Answer = 4 hours

We now need to work out the time it will take us to travel through the congestion zone. We know from the map that the distance inside the congestion zone is a total of 10 miles. We can only travel at a maximum speed of 5mph; therefore the calculation used to find out the total time it takes to travel through the congestion zone is as follows:

Time = Distance / Speed

Time = 10 / 5

Answer = 2 hours

All we need to do now is add the two travelling times together to reach a total of 6 hours travelling time.

ANSWER: Arrive at the hospital at 16:35hrs

PLANNING EXERCISE - LOGISTIC MAJESTIC

You are the dispatcher and driver for an Army Military Transport Unit based at UPSHOT BARRACKS (see attached map). Your normal operating hours are from 07:30 hours to whenever the last job is completed. However, this evening your Commanding Officer wants all members of the unit, in uniform, for a photograph at 17:05 hrs. Nonetheless, the unit directive requires that all requests for same-day transport received before 15:00 hours be met; after that time, tasks will be held over for the following day.

With 2 tasks left to complete today and the 15:00 hours deadline approaching, the telephone rings. A Royal Engineer, not affiliated to your unit is needed urgently at Garrick Barracks outside the town and he needs to take a large, bulky tank part with him. A lack of fuel, due to a petrol tanker drivers' strike, means that he can only get as far as your office so he needs onward travel; he will be with you any moment now and he expects to stay at Garrick barracks for 45 minutes. You already have a 150kg package to collect from one of your regular customers, a supply depot in RIGBY, to be delivered to the barracks next door to your office, and the wife of the Commanding Officer needs to be collected from home in HAMPTON by 15:25 hours to attend a civic reception in the Town Hall opposite the office at 15:45 hours. Due to other tasks, the only vehicles now available to you are an estate car similar to that used by the specialist engineer and with 30 litres of fuel in the tank, a small truck with 17 litres and a courier motorcycle complete with panniers with 9 litres. In addition to you there are 2 other drivers available. The previously mentioned petrol strike means no further fuel is available. The estate car can average 30 mph at 2½ miles/litre; the truck can average.

40 mph at 5 miles/litre and the motorcycle averages 50mph at 10miles/litre. You also know that major road-works south of the town will add 20 minutes to the direct journey between UPSHOT and RIGBY.

By the time you complete your plan and brief the other drivers it will be 15:00 hours. Find a solution that allows all tasks to be completed in the allotted time.

LOGISTIC MAJESTIC SKETCH MAP

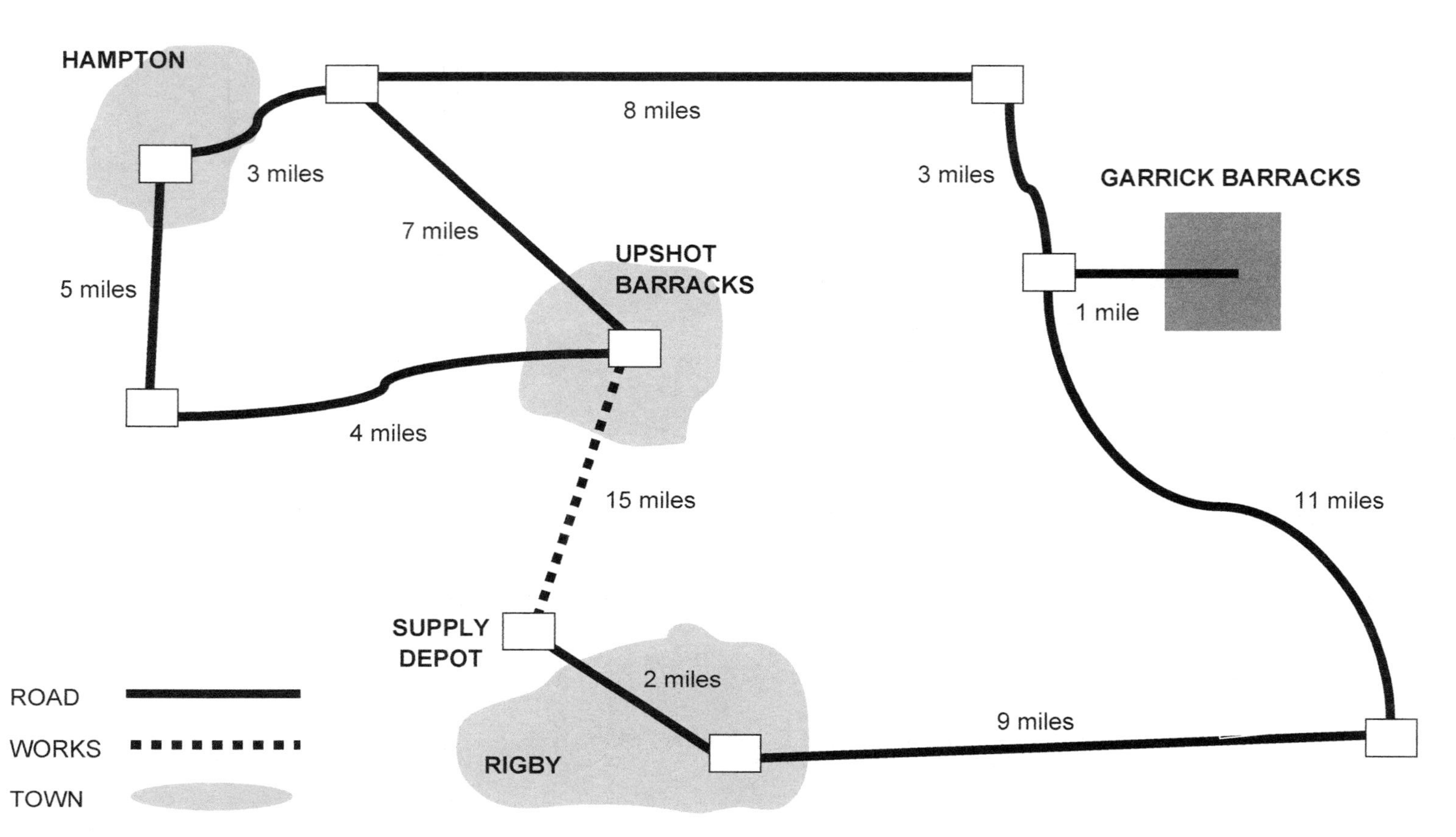
HAMPTON
3 miles
8 miles
3 miles
GARRICK BARRACKS
7 miles
UPSHOT
BARRACKS
5 miles
1 mile
4 miles
15 miles
11 miles
SUPPLY
DEPOT
2 miles
9 miles
RIGBY
ROAD
WORKS
TOWN

LOGISTIC MAJESTIC SOLUTIONS

IMPORTANT! The following solutions are just examples of a possible way to complete the tasks in hand. They do not represent the most efficient or quickest way to complete the exercise, and should be used for guidance only.

AIM

All tasks need to be completed and all personnel present for the unit photo at 1705 hours.

FACTORS & PLAN

Estate car's movements

Estate car to Commanding Officer's house ETD 15:00 (10 miles at 30 mph = 20 mins).

- ETA 15:20 and departs at same time for Town Hall (another 10 miles at 30mph = 20 mins).
- ETA 15:40 (5 mins to spare unless departure was delayed to 15:05).

Estate car now departs to Garrick Barracks ETD 15:40 (19 miles at 30 mph = 38 mins)

- ETA 16:18, collects Royal engineer

Estate car returns to unit (19 miles at 30 mph = 38 mins)

- ETA 16:56

Truck's movements

Truck to Garrick Barracks with Royal Engineer ETD 15:00 (19 miles at 40 mph = 28 mins)

- ETA 15:28 – Royal Engineer will be ready to depart at 16:13

Truck to supply depot (via South East route) (23 miles at 40 mph = 34 mins)

- ETD 15:28 for supply depot
- ETA and ETD supply depot 16:03

Truck return to barracks via road works (15 miles at 40 mph – 22 mins)

- Add 20 mins for roadworks
- ETA 16:45

Motorcycle

If the Royal Engineer has fitted bulky tank part and has no part to return, he could be collected by the motorcycle and would not, therefore have the 4 min wait at Garrick Barracks. However, even his tools might not fit in the panniers.

Motorcycle to Garrick Barracks (ETD as required) (but at 15:50 if there was no wait by either party) (19 miles at 50 mph = 23 mins)

- ETA 16:13

Motorcycle back to Upshot Barracks (19 miles at 50 mph = 23 mins)

- ETA 16:36

OTHER SOLUTIONS

One option would be to send the motorcycle to the Station Commander's house, the Estate car to the depot and the truck to Garrick Barracks, where it waits for the engineer. The Station Commander would not be very happy with his wife being on a motorcycle, though! All 3 drivers are also used, so there is no one to take the orders for tomorrow's tasks.

A second option would be to take the engineer to Garrick Barracks by truck, which then drives on to the supply depot, returning to Garrick to pick up the engineer up by reverse route. The estate car could then be used for the Commanding Officer's wife. However, the truck would be late arriving back (ETA 17:06) and you are under orders to be ready for the photograph by 17:05.

CHAPTER 7
HOW TO PASS THE AOSB INTERVIEWS

During this section of the guide we will provide you with a number of sample interview questions and advice on how to answer them. Whilst some of the questions will appear to be easy to answer, it is still important that we cover them, in order to ensure that you are fully prepared for your AOSB. We also recommend that you re-visit the ACA interview section of the guide, as some of the questions asked may be duplicated during the AOSB.

The sample questions have been divided into various sections to assist you during your preparation.

Section 1 - Personal/CV questions

Q. When and where were you born?

Q. Where are you living now and who are you living with?

Q. Where else have you lived apart from with your parents?

Q. Describe your home life to me?

Q. What was your life like growing up?

TIPS: Questions that relate to your home life are designed to assess how stable you are as person, whether or not you have any responsibilities at home, whether you are generally a happy person and also what you have learnt from life's experiences to date.

→ Try and provide examples of where you have moved around. This demonstrates that you are flexible and adaptable when the need arises.

→ It is preferable that your home life is stable.

→ The more responsibilities you have at home, such as washing, ironing, cleaning, financial responsibilities etc, the better.

→ If you have lived with other people, apart from your immediate family, tell them so. Remember – as an Army Officer you will be living with men and women of different ages.

Education

Q. How many schools have you attended and what years did you attend them?

Q. What did you think about your teachers?

Q. Tell me about your exam results; did you achieve the grades you wanted?

Q. Could you have worked harder whilst at school?

TIPS: Although these are relatively easy questions to respond to, ones that relate to your exam results and how hard you worked whilst at school could catch you out. You have to be honest about your results. If they were not up to the standard that you expected, have a valid reason why. Never be disrespectful of your teachers or the educational system. Remember that you are applying to join a disciplined service.

School/college

Q. Did you learn anything from other students?

Q. Did you have any responsibilities whilst at school or college?

Q. What sports did you participate in whilst at school or college?

Q. What clubs or societies were you a member of?

Q. Do you have the Duke of Edinburgh or similar awards?

Q. Where did you travel with school?

Q. Did you have any gaps in your education?

TIPS: If you did have any gaps in your education, it is better to say that you used the time wisely. Maybe you went travelling around the world in order to gain new experiences and cultures, or maybe you wanted to take time out from your studies to take on a work-related role or even a charity role. Whatever you do, do not say that you did nothing with your time off. If you went travelling, what did you gain from the experience?

Whilst at school or college it would be an advantage if you had some level of responsibility. For example, maybe you were a prefect or head of year, or maybe you were the captain of a sports team. You are applying to become an officer, which effectively means you are going to be a manager and a leader. Having some previous experience of these important roles will be an advantage. If you haven't had any responsibilities in your life to date, how do you know that you'll be a good leader or manager in the Army?

Outside interests and hobbies

Q. What sports are you currently engaged in?

Q. What sporting achievements have you gained?

Q. Have you been part of any youth organisations such as the Cadet, Scouts, Guides or Sea Cadets?

Q. Describe your hobbies and interests.

Q. Are you currently employed either full-time or part-time?

Q. What did you used to do during your school holidays?

Q. Have you ever travelled? If so, where and when did you go and what did you gain from the experience(s)?

Q. What are your future ambitions or plans?

TIPS: It is imperative that you demonstrate during the interview that you are an active person. If you sit at home all evening on your computer, playing games and surfing the net, then you are probably not the type of person the Army are looking for. Demonstrate to the interviewer that you are active, a team player and have hobbies and interests that challenge you both mentally and physically.

Employment

Q. What jobs have you had to date?

Q. What responsibilities did you have during each job?

Q. Why did you leave each job?

Q. Did you complete any courses or gain any qualifications during each job?

Q. Who did you have to communicate with in each job?

Q. Were you part of a team or did you work alone?

Q. What were your appraisals like?

TIPS: If you have no experience in a work-related role to date, how do you know that you will be a good employee for the Army? Make sure you have some work experience under your belt, even if it's part time work or charity work. Try to provide examples of responsibilities during each work role and any managerial experience too. These will all work in your favour.

Motivational questions

Q. Why do you want to join the Army? Have you considered the RAF or the Royal Navy?

Q. What specifically attracts you to the Army?

Q. When did you first want to join the Army and has anyone influenced you in your decision to join?

Q. Who have you talked to about a career in the Army?

Q. How many visits have you had to the Armed Forces Careers Office?

Q. Have you previously attended AOSB? If you have, what have you done to improve on last time?

Q. What contact have you had with the Army? Have you visited any establishments or spoken to any serving members?

Q. Are there any disadvantages to you joining?

Q. What do your family and friends think of you joining?

Q. What branch/regiment of the Army have you applied for?

Q. Would you consider any other branches/regiments of the Army other than the one(s) you have chosen?

Q. What research have you carried out during your preparation for joining the Army?

Q. Would you consider a Non-Commissioned role if you were unsuccessful at AOSB?

Q. What length of commission/service would you like to work?

Q. What qualities are required in order to become an Army Officer?

TIPS: Defend your Regiment choice as much as possible. In order to be capable of achieving this, you will need to know it inside out. Make sure you research key information about your chosen Regiment.

Knowledge of the Army

Q. Tell me what you know about the history of the Army?

Q. What training will you undergo as an Officer?

Q. Do you think you will have any problems or face any challenges during Officer Initial Training?

Q. Have you learnt anything about other branches of the Army?

Q. Tell me what you know about the different aircrafts that serve in the Army?

Q. Tell me what you know about the different types of weapons that the Army employs?

Q. How would you feel about going to war?

Q. Where are the UK bases of the Army?

Q. Whereabouts in the world are the Army operating right now?

Current affairs questions

Current affairs are a very important area of your preparation. You must carry out plenty of research in relation to current affairs. Not only will you need it during the interview(s), but it will also assist you during the essay element of the AOSB.

Here are a few important tips to help you research current affairs effectively:

TIP 1: Be careful what paper(s) you read. The type of paper you read will reflect you as a person. In the build up to AOSB, try reading the Times, or another quality newspaper.

TIP 2: We would strongly recommend that you subscribe to 'The Week'. This is a fantastic journal that will break down the week's stories for you. This will save you having to buy lots of different newspapers.

You can subscribe to the week at the following website:

www.theweek.co.uk

TIP 3: Consider reading the Economist. Once again, this is a quality journal that will provide you with lots of current affairs information.

You can subscribe to the Economist at the following website:

www.economist.com

TIP 4: Don't just research affairs that are relevant to the Army or the Armed Forces in general. Other topics are just as important!

The purpose of the current affairs section of the AOSB interview is designed to assess how informed you are of current global affairs. You should have a general view on each subject and have an understanding of why the issue is important. Try to have a general view of the whole world with knowledge of a number of issues and events.

Use this format to help you research news and current affairs events:

- What is the subject?
- Why is it significant?
- What is your opinion on it?

Sample current affairs questions

Q. Take me on a tour of the world and tell me what's caught your eye in the news recently.

Q. Tell me about 6 current affairs from abroad and six from home.

Q. Tell me about a news story from each continent.

USEFUL WEBSITES

BBC News: www.bbc.co.uk/news/

The Times Online: www.timesonline.co.uk

NATO (North Atlantic Treaty Organisation: www.nato.int

Ministry of Defence: www.mod.uk

Army: www.army.mod.uk

Royal Navy: www.royalnavy.mod.uk

Royal Air Force: www.raf.mod.uk

FINAL INTERVIEW TIPS

- Research key affairs from across the world.
- Have a broad knowledge of current affairs.
- Research affairs that have happened in the last 12 months.
- Focus in detail on events in the last 6 months.
- Select 6 topics for 'home' affairs (e.g. the budget, gang culture).
- Select 6 topics for 'away' affairs. Make sure that you use examples from right across the world.
- Gauge an opinion of each affair (you will need to be able to argue your point).
- Know key facts: people, numbers, locations etc.
- A firm handshake demonstrates a lot about your character.
- Be to the point and concise (don't waffle).
- Hold even eye contact with each boarding officer.
- Avoid hesitations such as "erm, ah, umm etc".
- Don't use slang.
- Sit up straight and don't slouch.
- Be confident but not overly so!
- Learn the dates and events listed on your application form.
- Make yourself stand out – do something different.
- Be aware of your weaknesses.
- Identify your strengths.
- Think before you speak.

CHAPTER 8
SAMPLE NUMERICAL, VERBAL & ABSTRACT REASONING TESTS

VERBAL REASONING – READING AND COMPREHENSION

For this section, you need to read the passage carefully and answer the questions that follow. For each question/statement, you need to determine whether it is true, false or impossible to say.

TRUE - If a statement is 'true', then it can be verified by the text. This means that the text must explicitly or implicitly mention something which proves the statement to be correct. In other words, you cannot make any assumptions about the text. There must either be direct evidence for the statement, or a strong inference to support the statement.

FALSE - If a statement is 'false', there must be evidence in the text which contradicts the statement. For example, if the question statement says 'all swans are white', but the text says 'there is such a thing as a black swan', then the statement is false because it is directly **contradicted by the text.**

CANNOT SAY - If there is not enough evidence to verify that the statement is true or false, then the correct answer is 'cannot say'. Simply put, this means that you cannot say the statement is true or false based on the information provided in the passage.

PRACTICE TEST 1

For the following questions, read the text before answering the questions as either TRUE, FALSE or CANNOT SAY from the information given.

ANALYSTS PROVE FORECASTERS WRONG

The Office for National Statistics (ONS) said internet shopping and sales of household goods had been better in October compared with previous months. However, sales of clothing and footwear, where many retailers cut prices before Christmas, were particularly weak.

The increase came as a surprise to many analysts who were predicting a 0.4% fall in internet shopping and sales of household goods. The rise meant that retail sale volumes in the three months leading up to January were up by 2.6% on the previous quarter. The final quarter of the year is a better guide to the underlying trend than one month's figures.

Some analysts cautioned that the heavy seasonal adjustment of the raw spending figures at the turn of the year made interpreting the data difficult. Even so, the government will be relieved that spending appears to be holding up despite the squeeze on incomes caused by high inflation, rising unemployment, a weak housing market and the crisis in the eurozone.

Retail sales account for less than half of total consumer spending and do not include the purchase of cars or eating out. The ONS said that its measure of inflation in the high street – the annual retail sales deflator – fell to 2.2% last month, its lowest level since November 2009. Ministers are hoping that lower inflation will boost real income growth during the course of 2012.

Q1a. Ministers hope that higher inflation will boost real income growth during 2012.

A - TRUE	B - FALSE	C - CANNOT SAY

Q1b. Analysts predicted a 0.4% rise in the sales of household goods.

A - TRUE	B - FALSE	C - CANNOT SAY

Q1c. The crisis in the eurozone is contributing to the squeeze on incomes.

A - TRUE	B - FALSE	C - CANNOT SAY

LONG-SERVICE PAYMENTS

Employees who attain fifteen years' continuous service between 7th November 2003 and 30th June 2007 shall qualify for the long-service payment at the rate applicable at the time. Employees who are promoted to a higher role during this period will cease to qualify for the payment but will receive a minimum pay increase on promotion of £300 per annum, which will be achieved through partial protection of the long-service payment.

Where the pay assimilation process on 7th November 2003 created a basic pay increase of more than 7%, and the employee was in receipt of the long-service payment, the payment has been reduced with effect from that date by the amount that the increase exceeded 7%. The consequent pay rates were set out in circular NJC/01/04.

PAY PROTECTION FOR EMPLOYEES ON THE RETAINED DUTY SYSTEM

Where an employee on the retained duty system has not received a pay increase of at least 7% (for the same pattern and level of activity) following full implementation of the pay award effective from 7th November 2003, the fire and rescue authority may introduce arrangements to ensure that such an increase is achieved.

Q2a. If an employee who is on the retained duty system has not received a pay increase of at least 7% following the implementation of the pay award, the fire and rescue service must introduce arrangements to ensure that such an increase is achieved.

A - TRUE	**B - FALSE**	**C - CANNOT SAY**

Q2b. Employees who attain fifteen years' continuous service between 7th November 2003 and 30th June 2008 shall qualify for the long-service payment at the rate applicable at the time.

A - TRUE	**B - FALSE**	**C - CANNOT SAY**

Q2c. The pay assimilation process on 7th November 2003 created a basic pay increase for all employees of more than 7%.

A - TRUE	**B - FALSE**	**C - CANNOT SAY**

DATA WAREHOUSES

A data warehouse is the main source of information for an organisation's historical data. Its historical data is often referred to as its corporate memory. As an example of how a data warehouse can be put to good use, an organisation would use the information stored in its data warehouse to find out how many particular stock items they sold on a particular day in a particular year. They could also ascertain which employees were off sick on any given day or any given year. The data stored within the warehouse contains essential information so that managers can make appropriate management decisions.

A data warehouse is normally large in size as the information stored usually focuses on basic, structured and organised data. Some of the characteristics of the data in a data warehouse are as follows:

Time-variant - changes to the data in the database are tracked and recorded so that reports can be produced showing changes over time;

Non-volatile - the data in the database is never over-written or deleted but is retained for future reporting;

Integrated - the database contains data from most or all of an organisation's operational applications. This data is useful and meaningful for further processing and analysis.

Q3a. Integrated and non-volatile data form some of the characteristics of a data warehouse.

A - TRUE	B - FALSE	C - CANNOT SAY

Q3b. It is not possible to identify which employees were on sick leave from the information stored in a data warehouse.

A - TRUE	B - FALSE	C - CANNOT SAY

Q3c. Corporate memory is an alternative name given to historical data.

A - TRUE	B - FALSE	C - CANNOT SAY

THE IMPORTANCE OF HEALTH AND SAFETY IN THE WORKPLACE

Employers must protect the health and safety of everyone in your workplace, including people with disabilities, and provide welfare facilities for your employees.

Basic things you need to consider are outlined below.

WELFARE FACILITIES

For your employees' well-being you need to provide:

- Toilets and hand basins, with soap and towels or a hand-dryer, drinking water.
- A place to store clothing (and somewhere to change if special clothing is worn for work).
- Somewhere to rest and eat meals.

HEALTH ISSUES

To have a healthy working environment, make sure there is:

- Good ventilation – a supply of fresh, clean air drawn from outside or a ventilation system.
- A reasonable working temperature (usually at least 16°C, or 13°C for strenuous work, unless other laws require lower temperatures).
- Lighting suitable for the work being carried out.
- Enough room space and suitable workstations and seating.
- A clean workplace with appropriate waste containers.

Q4a. It is the responsibility of the employee for keeping a workplace safe.

A - TRUE	B - FALSE	C - CANNOT SAY

Q4b. Providing the employee with a suitable workstation is a consideration for the employer when making the workplace safe.

A - TRUE	B - FALSE	C - CANNOT SAY

Q4c. An employer must ensure that all floor surfaces are non-slip in order to prevent slips, trips and falls.

A - TRUE	B - FALSE	C - CANNOT SAY

MAGISTRATE TRAINING

The entire selection process for becoming a magistrate can take approximately 12 months, sometimes longer depending on the area.

Once you have been accepted you will be required to undertake a comprehensive training course which is usually held over a 3-day period (18 hours). During this course you will learn the necessary skills that are required in order to become a magistrate.

The training is normally carried out by the Justice Clerk who is responsible for the court. He/she will usually be the legal advisor during your magistrate sittings. They will help you to develop all the necessary skills required in order to carry out your duties professionally and competently.

You will carry out your training as part of a group with other people who have been recruited at the same time as you. This is extremely beneficial as it will allow you to learn in a safe environment.

Training will be given using a variety of methods, which may include pre- course reading, small-group work, use of case studies, computer-based training and CCTV. It is recognised that magistrates are volunteers and that their time is valuable, so every effort is made to provide all training at times and places convenient to trainees. The Ministry of Justice booklet 'Serving as a Magistrate' has more information about the magistracy and the role of magistrates.

Q5a. The comprehensive training course for becoming a magistrate usually consists of 3 days, divided into 6 hours training per day.

A - TRUE	B - FALSE	C - CANNOT SAY

Q5b. An applicant can find out more about the role of a magistrate by reading the Ministry of Justice booklet 'Serving as a Magistrate'.

A - TRUE	B - FALSE	C - CANNOT SAY

Q5c. The selection process for becoming a magistrate will take no longer than 12 months.

A - TRUE	B - FALSE	C - CANNOT SAY

ANSWERS TO PRACTICE TEST 1

ANALYSTS PROVE FORECASTERS WRONG

The Office for National Statistics (ONS) said internet shopping and sales of household goods had been better in October compared with previous months. However, sales of clothing and footwear, where many retailers cut prices before Christmas, were particularly weak.

[b]: The increase came as a surprise to many analysts who were predicting a 0.4% fall in internet shopping and sales of household goods. The rise meant that retail sale volumes in the three months leading up to January were up by 2.6% on the previous quarter. The final quarter of the year is a better guide to the underlying trend than one month's figures.

Some analysts cautioned that the heavy seasonal adjustment of the raw spending figures at the turn of the year made interpreting the data difficult. Even so, the government will be relieved that spending appears to be holding up [c]: despite the squeeze on incomes caused by high inflation, rising unemployment, a weak housing market and the crisis in the eurozone.

Retail sales account for less than half of total consumer spending and do not include the purchase of cars or eating out. The ONS said that its measure of inflation in the high street – the annual retail sales deflator – fell to 2.2% last month, its lowest level since November 2009. [a]: Ministers are hoping that lower inflation will boost real income growth during the course of 2012.

Q1a. Ministers hope that higher inflation will boost real income growth during 2012.

Answer - B (FALSE) The passage states that ministers hope that 'lower' inflation will boost real income growth, not higher. Therefore, the statement is false.

Q1b. Analysts predicted a 0.4% rise in the sales of household goods.

Answer - B (FALSE) The passage states that analysts were predicting a 0.4% fall in sales of household goods, not rise. Therefore, the statement is false.

Q1c. The crisis in the eurozone is contributing to the squeeze on incomes.

Answer - A (TRUE) This statement is true based on the information provided in the passage.

LONG-SERVICE PAYMENTS

[b]: Employees who attain fifteen years' continuous service between 7th November 2003 and 30th June 2007 shall qualify for the long-service payment at the rate applicable at the time. Employees who are promoted to a higher role during this period will cease to qualify for the payment but will receive a minimum pay increase on promotion of £300 per annum, which will be achieved through partial protection of the long-service payment.

Where the pay assimilation process on 7th November 2003 created a basic pay increase of more than 7%, and the employee was in receipt of the long-service payment, the payment has been reduced with effect from that date by the amount that the increase exceeded 7%. The consequent pay rates were set out in circular NJC/01/04.

PAY PROTECTION FOR EMPLOYEES ON THE RETAINED DUTY SYSTEM

[a]: Where an employee on the retained duty system has not received a pay increase of at least 7% (for the same pattern and level of activity) following full implementation of the pay award effective from 7th November 2003, the fire and rescue authority may introduce arrangements to ensure that such an increase is achieved.

ACTING UP AND TEMPORARY PROMOTION

The NJC recognises that in the early stages of implementing the Integrated Personal Development System it may, on occasions, be difficult to apply the principles at Paragraph 19 of Section 4 Part B. Fire and rescue authorities, employees and trade unions should therefore adopt a co-operative and common sense approach to any problems that might arise.

Q2a. If an employee who is on the retained duty system has not received a pay increase of at least 7% following the implementation of the pay award, the fire and rescue service must introduce arrangements to ensure that such an increase is achieved.

Answer - B (FALSE) This statement is false because the sentence states that the fire and rescue service 'may' introduce arrangements; it does not say they 'must'.

Q2b. Employees who attain fifteen years' continuous service between 7th November 2003 and 30th June 2008 shall qualify for the long-service payment at the rate applicable at the time.

Answer - B (FALSE) This statement is false because the sentence states 30th June 2008, instead of 30th June 2007 as stated in the passage.

Q2c. The pay assimilation process on 7th November 2003 created a basic pay increase for all employees of more than 7%.

Answer - C (CANNOT SAY) We cannot say that this statement is true or false. It makes no reference in the passage that 'all' employees received a pay rise.

DATA WAREHOUSES

A data warehouse is the main source of information for an organisation's historical data. [c]: Its historical data is often referred to as its corporate memory. As an example of how a data warehouse can be put to good use, an organisation would use the information stored in its data warehouse to find out how many particular stock items they sold on a particular day in a particular year. [b]: They could also ascertain which employees were off sick on any given day or any given year. The data stored within the warehouse contains essential information so that managers can make appropriate management decisions.

A data warehouse is normally large in size as the information stored usually focuses on basic, structured and organised data. [a]: Some of the characteristics of the data in a data warehouse are as follows:

Time-variant - changes to the data in the database are tracked and recorded so that reports can be produced showing changes over time;

Non-volatile - the data in the database is never over-written or deleted but is retained for future reporting;

Integrated - the database contains data from most or all of an organisation's operational applications. This data is useful and meaningful for further processing and analysis.

Q3a. Integrated and non-volatile data form some of the characteristics of a data warehouse.

Answer - A (TRUE) It is true, according to the passage, that some of the characteristics of a data warehouse include integrated and non-volatile data.

Q3b. It is not possible to identify which employees were on sick leave from the information stored in a data warehouse.

Answer - B (FALSE) It is possible to ascertain which employees were off sick from the information stored in a data warehouse; therefore, the statement is false.

Q3c. Corporate memory is an alternative name given to historical data.

Answer - A (TRUE) It is true that corporate memory is an alternative name given to historical data.

THE IMPORTANCE OF HEALTH AND SAFETY IN THE WORKPLACE

You must protect the safety and health of everyone in your workplace, including people with disabilities, and provide welfare facilities for your employees.

Basic things you need to consider are outlined below.

WELFARE FACILITIES

For your employees' well-being you need to provide:

- Toilets and hand basins, with soap and towels or a hand-dryer, drinking water.
- A place to store clothing (and somewhere to change if special clothing is worn for work).
- Somewhere to rest and eat meals.

HEALTH ISSUES

To have a healthy working environment, make sure there is:

- Good ventilation – a supply of fresh, clean air drawn from outside or a ventilation system.
- A reasonable working temperature (usually at least 16°C, or 13°C for strenuous work, unless other laws require lower temperatures).
- Lighting suitable for the work being carried out.
- [b]: Enough room space and suitable workstations and seating.
- A clean workplace with appropriate waste containers.

Q4a. It is the responsibility of the employee for keeping a workplace safe.

Answer - C (CANNOT SAY) The passage makes no reference to this statement. Therefore, we cannot say whether the statement is true or false from the information provided. Cannot say is the correct answer.

Q4b. Providing the employee with a suitable workstation is a consideration for the employer when making the workplace safe.

Answer - A (TRUE) We can deduce from the passage that this statement is true.

Q4c. An employer must ensure that all floor surfaces are non-slip in order to prevent slips, trips and falls.

Answer - C (CANNOT SAY) In health and safety law this statement is true. However, the passage makes no reference it. Cannot say is the correct answer.

MAGISTRATE TRAINING

[c]: The entire selection process for becoming a magistrate can take approximately 12 months, sometimes longer depending on the area.

[a]: Once you have been accepted you will be required to undertake a comprehensive training course which is usually held over a 3-day period (18 hours). During this course you will learn the necessary skills that are required in order to become a magistrate.

The training is normally carried out by the Justice Clerk who is responsible for the court. He/she will usually be the legal advisor during your magistrate sittings. They will help you to develop all the necessary skills required in order to carry out your duties professionally and competently.

You will carry out your training as part of a group with other people who have been recruited at the same time as you. This is extremely beneficial as it will allow you to learn in a safe environment.

Training will be given using a variety of methods, which may include precourse reading, small-group work, use of case studies, computer-based training and CCTV. It is recognised that magistrates are volunteers and that their time is valuable, so every effort is made to provide all training at times and places convenient to trainees. [b]: The Ministry of Justice booklet 'Serving as a Magistrate' has more information about the magistracy and the role of magistrates.

Q5a. The comprehensive training course for becoming a magistrate usually consists of 3 days, divided into 6 hours training per day.

Answer - C (CANNOT SAY) The passage does state that the training course is usually held over a 3-day period (18 hours). We could assume that the 18 hours are equally divided into 3 × 6 hour days. However, it is not our job to assume; we must base our answers on what is provided within the passage. Therefore, the correct answer is cannot say.

Q5b. An applicant can find out more about the role of a magistrate by reading the Ministry of Justice booklet 'Serving as a Magistrate'.

Answer - A (TRUE) From the passage we know this statement to be true.

Q5c. The selection process for becoming a magistrate will take no longer than 12 months.

Answer - B (FALSE) This statement is false because the passage states that the selection process can sometimes take longer than 12 months.

PRACTICE TEST 2

LEARNING THE TRAIN DRIVER'S ROUTE KNOWLEDGE

Competence in the train driver's route knowledge is extremely important, simply because trains have such a long stopping distance. As an example, a train travelling at a speed of 200 km/h can take three miles to stop. If the driver lacks route knowledge, then stopping distances can be compromised. Stopping distances can be greatly affected by the weight of a train. Trains cannot be driven on line-of-sight like road vehicles because the driver has to know what is up-ahead in order to operate the train safely. This is why route knowledge is so important to the role of a train driver.

During initial training a trainee driver will be given a Route Learning Ticket. This gives the driver authority to travel in the cab whilst they learn the routes under supervision of a qualified instructor or qualified train driver. However, visual aids such as videos and visual learning platforms are being introduced so that drivers can learn the routes in a more controlled environment.

In order to successfully pass the route knowledge assessment a driver must learn all of the stations, speed restrictions, signals, signal boxes, level crossings, gradients and other features that are applicable to the role.

The assessment is either with a question and answer session in front of the manager or with a multiple choice route assessment package on a computer.

Q1a. A train's stopping distance is increased by the weight of the train.

A - TRUE	B - FALSE	C - CANNOT SAY

Q1b. A train travelling at a speed of 400 km/h will take six miles to stop.

A - TRUE	B - FALSE	C - CANNOT SAY

Q1c. Learning speed restrictions and stations will help towards passing the route knowledge assessment.

A - TRUE	B - FALSE	C - CANNOT SAY

SENDING FRANKED MAIL

You have the option of a one-off collection or a regular daily collection at a pre-arranged time. You can print and complete the form for a regular collection, or if you require a one-off collection or wish to discuss your collection requirements in more detail you can call the Business Relations Manager.

If you need to carry out an urgent same day mailing and would like your mail collected, you'll need to let us know before 12.00pm the same day by calling the Business Support telephone number. We will then arrange a single collection from your premises.

WEEKEND COLLECTIONS

We cannot collect on Saturdays or Sundays without prior arrangement. If you are interested in arranging a weekend collection for your business then please contact your allocated business support manager. A turnover in excess of £2500 per annum is required for this service. Any franked mail inaccuracies will be rejected.

PREPARING FRANKED MAIL FOR COLLECTION

1. Be sure to address your mail correctly, using the correct postcode and postage.
2. Bundle all franked mail together, with the addresses facing the same direction.
3. Bundle different types of mail separately.
4. Put stamped mail in separate bags.
5. Weigh each pouch, bag or tray, checking that they're less than 11kg (to comply with the health and safety limit).
6. Check that all your mail is ready for collection on time and at your collection point.

Q2a. Saturday collections can be arranged with prior arrangement.

A - TRUE	B - FALSE	C - CANNOT SAY

Q2b. The health and safety limit for a bag of mail is less than 11kg.

A - TRUE	B - FALSE	C - CANNOT SAY

Q2c. Bundled franked mail with the addresses that are not facing the same direction will be rejected.

A - TRUE	B - FALSE	C - CANNOT SAY

BUSINESS FRANCHISE INFORMATION

Franchises are very popular at the moment with increasing numbers of people choosing to buy one as opposed to starting out by setting up their own business. By purchasing a franchise you are effectively taking advantage of the success of an already established business. As the 'franchisee', you are buying a licence to use the name, products, services, and management support systems of the "franchiser" company. This licence normally covers a particular geographical area and runs for a limited time. The downside to a franchise is that you will never actually legally own the business.

As a franchisee, the way you pay for the franchise may be through an initial fee, ongoing management fees, a share of your turnover, or a combination of these depending on how you have set up the franchise. A franchise business can take different legal forms - most are sole traders, partnerships or limited companies. Whatever the structure, the franchisee's freedom to manage the business is limited by the terms of the franchise agreement.

There is information to suggest that the franchise business sector is still growing rapidly. During 2007 the Natwest Bank carried out a survey into the UK franchise market which revealed the astonishing financial growth of this sector. The approximate annual turnover of the business franchise sector is in excess of £10.8 billion.

What is more interesting to note is that the vast majority of business franchisees in 2007 were in profit - a total of 93% to be exact. In 1991 the total number of profitable franchisees was 70% and in 2004 it was 88%. Therefore, this business sector is growing.

Q3a. During 2007 the total number of business franchises that were not in profit totalled 7%.

A - TRUE	B - FALSE	C - CANNOT SAY

Q3b. As the 'franchiser', you are buying a licence to use the name, products, services, and management support systems of the 'franchisee' company.

A - TRUE	B - FALSE	C - CANNOT SAY

Q3c. A franchise business can take different legal forms including Limited Liability Partnership (LLP).

A - TRUE	B - FALSE	C - CANNOT SAY

COMPANY ORDERING PROCESS

1.1 Our display of products and online services on our website is an invitation and not an offer to sell those goods to you.

1.2 An offer is made when you place the order for your products or online service. However, we will not have made a contract with you unless and until we accept your offer.

1.3 We take payment from your card when we process your order and have checked your card details. Goods are subject to availability. If we are unable to supply the goods, we will inform you of this as soon as possible. A full refund will be given if you have already paid for the goods. It is our aim to always keep our website updated and all goods displayed available.

1.4 If you enter a correct email address we will send you an order acknowledgement email immediately and receipt of payment. These do not constitute an order confirmation or order acceptance from us.

1.5 Unless we have notified you that we do not accept your order or you have cancelled it, order acceptance and the creation of the contract between you and us will take place at the point the goods you have ordered are dispatched.

1.6 The contract will be formed at the place of dispatch of the goods. All goods, wherever possible, will be dispatched within 24 hours of the order being placed, Monday to Thursday. If your order falls on a weekend or bank holiday, your order will be dispatched on the next available working day. All orders that are sent via recorded delivery will require a signature. In the majority of cases, however, we will dispatch goods using Royal Mail's standard First Class delivery service.

Q4a. If a customer places an order, and they have entered a correct email address, they will immediately receive an order confirmation email.

A - TRUE	B - FALSE	C - CANNOT SAY

Q4b. Orders placed on a Friday will be dispatched on a Saturday.

A - TRUE	B - FALSE	C - CANNOT SAY

Q4c. Payment is taken from the card once the card details have been checked.

A - TRUE	B - FALSE	C - CANNOT SAY

THE HISTORY OF FOOTBALL

The earliest records of a game similar to football as we know it today are from China in 206 BC. By AD 500, round footballs stuffed with hair were in use. It is suggested that Roman legions may have introduced the game to Europe and England in particular during the Roman occupation from AD 40 to AD 400.

The game increased in popularity, developing into 'mob games' called mêlées, or mellays, in which a ball, usually an inflated animal bladder, was advanced by kicking, punching and carrying. As many as 100 players from two towns or parishes started at a mid-point and used their localities' limits as goals. King Richard II of England banned the game in 1389 because it interfered with archery practice, and later monarchs issued similar proscriptions into the 15th century, to little effect.

By the middle of the 19th century it was decided that uniformity of the rules was necessary so that every team could play the same game. Therefore the Football Association (FA) was formed in England and during the latter part of 1863, following a series of meetings, the first rules of the game of football were laid down. The first rules were based on those that had been in use at Cambridge University at the time. Some of the first rules also known as the Laws of the Game (there were 14 in total) included:

Rule 1. The maximum length of the ground shall be 200 yards; the maximum breadth shall be 100 yards; the length and breadth shall be marked off with flags; and the goals shall be defined by two upright posts, 8 yards apart, without any tape or bar across them.

Rule 10. Neither tripping nor hacking shall be allowed, and no player shall use his hands to hold or push an adversary.

Q5a. By the middle of the 19th century it was decided that uniforms would be worn by referees.

A - TRUE	B - FALSE	C - CANNOT SAY

Q5b. King Richard II of England practised archery.

A - TRUE	B - FALSE	C - CANNOT SAY

Q5c. According to the passage there were four Laws of the Game.

A - TRUE	B - FALSE	C - CANNOT SAY

ANSWERS TO PRACTICE TEST 2

LEARNING THE TRAIN DRIVER'S ROUTE KNOWLEDGE

Competence in the train driver's route knowledge is extremely important, simply because trains have such a long stopping distance. [b]: As an example, a train travelling at a speed of 200 km/h can take three miles to stop. If the driver lacks route knowledge, then stopping distances can be compromised. [a]: Stopping distances can be greatly affected by the weight of a train. Trains cannot be driven on line- of-sight like road vehicles because the driver has to know what is up ahead in order to operate the train safely. This is why route knowledge is so important to the role of a train driver.

During initial training a trainee driver will be given a Route Learning Ticket. This gives the driver authority to travel in the cab whilst they learn the routes under supervision with a qualified instructor or qualified train driver. However, visual aids such as videos and visual learning platforms are being introduced so that drivers can learn the routes in a more controlled environment.

[c]: In order to successfully pass the route knowledge assessment a driver must learn all of the stations, speed restrictions, signals, signal boxes, level crossings, gradients and other features that are applicable to the role.

The assessment is either with a question and answer session in front of the manager or with a multiple choice route assessment package on a computer.

Q1a. A train's stopping distance is increased by the weight of the train.

Answer - C (CANNOT SAY) Whilst common sense would dictate that a train's stopping distance will increase by its weight we can only answer the question based on information provided. The passage states that stopping distances can be greatly affected by weight; however, it does not confirm that the stopping distance is increased by the weight. Therefore, we must choose cannot say.

Q1b. A train travelling at a speed of 400 km/h will take six miles to stop.

Answer - C (CANNOT SAY) The passage states that a train travelling at a speed of 200km/h can take three miles to stop. You could be forgiven for assuming that a train travelling at 400 km/h would take six miles to stop. However, the passage does not confirm this and therefore we must select cannot say as the correct answer.

Q1c. Learning speed restrictions and stations will help towards passing the route knowledge assessment.

Answer - A (TRUE) This is made clear by the third paragraph.

SENDING FRANKED MAIL

You have the option of a one-off collection or a regular daily collection at a pre-arranged time. You can print and complete the form for a regular collection, or if you require a one-off collection or wish to discuss your collection requirements in more detail you can call the Business Relations Manager.

If you need to carry out an urgent same day mailing and would like your mail collected, you'll need to let us know before 12.00pm the same day by calling the Business Support telephone number. We will then arrange a single collection from your premises.

WEEKEND COLLECTIONS

[a]: We cannot collect on Saturdays or Sundays without prior arrangement. If you are interested in arranging a weekend collection for your business then please contact your allocated business support manager. A turnover in excess of £2500 per annum is required for this service. Any franked mail inaccuracies will be rejected.

PREPARING FRANKED MAIL FOR COLLECTION

1. Be sure to address your mail correctly, using the correct postcode and postage.
2. [c]: Bundle all franked mail together, with the addresses facing the same direction.
3. Bundle different types of mail separately.
4. Put stamped mail in separate bags.
5. [b]: Weigh each pouch, bag or tray, checking that they're less than 11kg (to comply with the health and safety limit).
6. Check that all your mail is ready for collection on time and at your collection point.

Q2a. Saturday collections can be arranged with prior arrangement.

Answer - A (TRUE) The passage states that they cannot collect on Saturdays or Sundays without prior arrangement. Therefore, the statement is true.

Q2b. The health and safety limit for a bag of mail is less than 11kg.

Answer - A (TRUE) The passage indicates that less than 11kg is the health and safety limit; therefore, the correct answer is true.

Q2c. Bundled franked mail with the addresses that are not facing the same direction will be rejected.

Answer - A (TRUE) In paragraph 3 of the passage it states that any franked mail inaccuracies will be rejected. The statement is true.

BUSINESS FRANCHISE INFORMATION

Franchises are very popular at the moment with increasing numbers of people choosing to buy one as opposed to starting out by setting up their own business. By purchasing a franchise you are effectively taking advantage of the success of an already established business. [b]: As the 'franchisee', you are buying a licence to use the name, products, services, and management support systems of the 'franchiser' company. This licence normally covers a particular geographical area and runs for a limited time. The downside to a franchise is that you will never actually legally own the business.

As a franchisee, the way you pay for the franchise may be through an initial fee, ongoing management fees, a share of your turnover, or a combination of these depending on how you have set up the franchise. [c]: A franchise business can take different legal forms - most are sole traders, partnerships or limited companies. Whatever the structure, the franchisee's freedom to manage the business is limited by the terms of the franchise agreement.

There is information to suggest that the franchise business sector is still growing rapidly. During 2007 the Natwest Bank carried out a survey into the UK franchise market which revealed the astonishing financial growth of this sector. The approximate annual turnover of the business franchise sector is in excess of £10.8 billion. [a]: What is more interesting to note is that the vast majority of business franchisees in 2007 were in profit - a total of 93% to be exact. In 1991 the total number of profitable franchisees was 70% and in 2004 it was 88%. Therefore, this business sector is growing.

Q3a. During 2007 the total number of business franchises that were not in profit totalled 7%.

Answer - A (TRUE) The passage states that 93% of business franchises in 2007 were in profit. This means that 7% were not in profit. The correct answer is true.

Q3b. As the 'franchiser', you are buying a licence to use the name, products, services, and management support systems of the 'franchisee' company.

Answer - B (FALSE) The passage states "As the 'franchisee', you are buying a licence to use the name, products, services, and management support systems of the 'franchiser' company". The correct answer is false.

Q3c. A franchise business can take different legal forms including Limited Liability Partnership (LLP).

Answer - C (CANNOT SAY) We cannot state whether this sentence is true or false from the information provided. The passage states only that "a franchise business can take different legal forms". We cannot assume that this includes Limited Liability Partnerships (LLP). The correct answer is cannot say.

COMPANY ORDERING PROCESS

1.1 Our display of products and online services on our website is an invitation and not an offer to sell those goods to you.

1.2 An offer is made when you place the order for your products or online service. However, we will not have made a contract with you unless and until we accept your offer.

1.3 [c]: We take payment from your card when we process your order and have checked your card details. Goods are subject to availability. If we are unable to supply the goods, we will inform you of this as soon as possible. A full refund will be given if you have already paid for the goods. It is our aim to always keep our website updated and all goods displayed available.

1.4 [a]: If you enter a correct email address we will send you an order acknowledgement email immediately and receipt of payment. These do not constitute an order confirmation or order acceptance from us.

1.5 Unless we have notified you that we do not accept your order or you have cancelled it, order acceptance and the creation of the contract between you and us will take place at the point the goods you have ordered are dispatched.

1.6 [b]: The contract will be formed at the place of dispatch of the goods. All goods, wherever possible, will be dispatched within 24 hours of the order being placed, Monday to Thursday. If your order falls on a weekend or bank holiday, your order will be dispatched on the next available working day. All orders that are sent via recorded delivery will require a signature. In the majority of cases, however, we will dispatch goods using Royal Mail's standard First Class delivery service.

Q4a. If a customer places an order, and they have entered a correct email address, they will immediately receive an order confirmation email.

Answer - B (FALSE) The passage states that if a correct email address is entered they will send the customer an order acknowledgment email. It goes on to state that this email is not an order confirmation. The correct answer is false.

Q4b. Orders placed on a Friday will be dispatched on a Saturday.

Answer - C (CANNOT SAY) The passage states "If your order falls on a weekend or bank holiday, your order will be dispatched on the next available working day". Although we could assume that the next 'working day' is Monday, this cannot be confirmed by the text in the passage.

Q4c. Payment is taken from the card once the card details have been checked.

Answer - A (TRUE) From the information provided in the passage we can confirm that this sentence is true.

THE HISTORY OF FOOTBALL

The earliest records of a game similar to football as we know it today are from China in 206 BC. By AD 500, round footballs stuffed with hair were in use. It is suggested that Roman legions may have introduced the game to Europe and England in particular during the Roman occupation from AD 40 to AD 400.

The game increased in popularity, developing into 'mob games' called mêlées, or mellays, in which a ball, usually an inflated animal bladder, was advanced by kicking, punching and carrying. As many as 100 players from two towns or parishes started at a mid-point and used their localities' limits as goals. [b]: King Richard II of England banned the game in 1389 because it interfered with archery practice, and later monarchs issued similar proscriptions into the 15th century, to little effect.

[a]: By the middle of the 19th century it was decided that uniformity of the rules was necessary so that every team could play the same game. Therefore the Football Association (FA) was formed in England and dur- ing the latter part of 1863, following a series of meetings, the first rules of the game of football were laid down. The first rules were based on those that had been in use at Cambridge University at the time. [c]: Some of the first rules also known as the Laws of the Game (there were 14 in total) included:

Rule 1. The maximum length of the ground shall be 200 yards; the maximum breadth shall be 100 yards; the length and breadth shall be marked off with flags; and the goals shall be defined by two upright posts, 8 yards apart, without any tape or bar across them.

Rule 10. Neither tripping nor hacking shall be allowed, and no player shall use his hands to hold or push an adversary.

Q5a. By the middle of the 19th century it was decided that uniforms would be worn by referees.

Answer - C (CANNOT SAY) Although the passage makes reference to the 19th century and unifor- mity, it does not make reference to referees wearing uniforms. The correct answer is cannot say from the information provided.

Q5b. King Richard II of England practised archery.

Answer - C (CANNOT SAY) This is a tricky one that may catch some people out! The passage states that King Richard II of England banned the game in 1389 because it interfered with archery practice. However, the passage does not state that it was he who practised archery. Therefore, the correct answer is cannot say.

Q5c. According to the passage there were four Laws of the Game.

Answer - B (FALSE) The sentence is false. The passage states that there were fourteen Laws of the Game.

NUMERICAL REASONING

Numerical reasoning is fairly simple in application, but much harder in practice. All you need to do is answer the mathematical based questions listed in the test. In order to do this, you'll need to demonstrate ability in standard mathematical applications, such as addition and subtraction, and work out the relationship between figures in sets of data. Have a go at the questions below and see how you get on.

PRACTICE TEST 1

QUESTION 1

You leave your house at 10:05. You travel for half an hour at 50 mph. When you reach the motorway, the traffic forces you to drive at 15 mph for 12 minutes. After the traffic clears, you continue your journey at 50 mph and arrive at your destination at 11:25.

1. Approximately, how far do you travel in total?

A	B	C	D
80 miles	60 miles	20 miles	30 miles

2. How long does the third part of your journey take?

A	B	C	D
38 minutes	22 minutes	50 minutes	44 minutes

3. How long would you have been travelling for if you had not got stuck in traffic, assuming you remained at 50 mph for the whole journey?

A	B	C	D
1 hour and 2 minutes	1 hour and 5 minutes	1 hour and 15 minutes	1 hour and 12 minutes

QUESTION 2

Below are diagrams of two different parks. The diagrams show the layout of each park. The sizes of each park are labelled in metres.

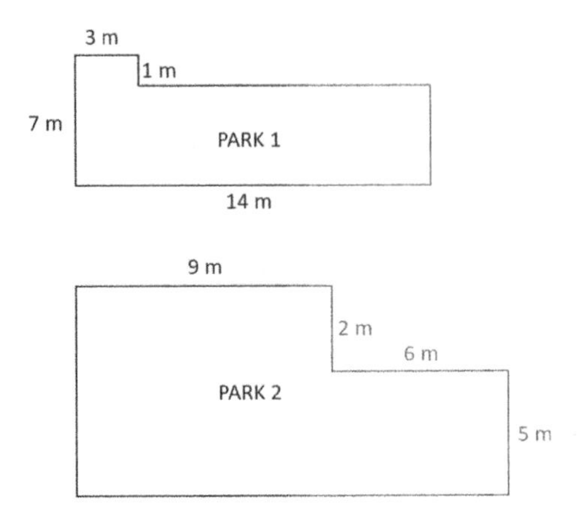

1. In square metres, work out the total area of Park 1.

A	B	C	D
82 sq m	91 sq m	75 sq m	87 sq m

2. Work out the difference between Park 1 and Park 2 total area.

A	B	C	D
7 sq m	6 sq m	5 sq m	12 sq m

3. Approximately, what percentage of the total of both parks' areas is covered by Park 1?

A	B	C	D
53%	52%	48%	50%

QUESTION 3

A company has a store made up of confectionary, savoury and drinks. 14%, or 70 items, are confectionary. The ratio of drinks to confectionary is 1 to 3.5.

1. How many drinks are there in the store?

A	B	C	D
20	30	25	40

2. In total, how many items are there in the store?

A	B	C	D
480	500	620	580

3. How many savoury items are in the store?

A	B	C	D
350	90	410	220

QUESTION 4

A local gym holds different classes throughout the week.

MON	TUES	WED	THURS	FRI	SAT	SUN
Aerobics	Legs, Bums and Tums	Swimming (Beginners)	Hula Hooping	Boxercise	Circuits	Swimming
Circuits	Aerobics	Legs, Bums and Tums	Kick Boxing	Swimming	Swimming	Aerobics
Cycling	Kettlebell	Latin Dancing	Swimming	Legs, Bums, and Tums	Cycling	Boxercise

1. During the weekdays, if each class lasted 90 minutes, how long in total are classes conducted for? Give your answer in hours and minutes.

A	B	C	D
30 hours	24 hours and 30 minutes	22 hours and 30 minutes	23 hours and 45 minutes

2. Based on the seven days, what is the ratio of swimming classes to legs, bums and tums classes?

A	B	C	D
3:5	2:1	4:2	5:3

3. If you wanted to join the gym, a new membership costs £14.99 per month, with a contract for a minimum of 3 months. Classes are an additional £2.50. Assuming you had your contract for the minimum time, and attended 8 classes in total, how much will that cost you in total?

A	B	C	D
£71.82	£64.97	£69.54	£72.50

QUESTION 5

A Christmas bonus is being offered to the employee who secures the most number of sales across the next 20-day working period.

The Christmas bonus will be an additional 20% of an employee's wages. The company are using this new incentive as a way of boosting sales during their peak time. The Managing Director says that this bonus incentive will continue each year, if it proves to be successful.

The table below shows the top six employees' sale results recorded weekly (5 working days).

NAME	TOM	DAVE	MARY	ALICIA	LOGAN	MILLIE
Week 1	3	4	0	3	4	6
Week 2	2	1	5	2	3	1
Week 3	4	6	2	4	4	5
Week 4	0	4	2	1	3	0

1. Which employee will receive the Christmas bonus?

A	B	C	D	E	F
Tom	Dave	Mary	Alicia	Logan	Millie

2. If the employee who receives the Christmas bonus earns £1,500 that month, what will their total wages be including the Christmas bonus?

A	B	C	D
£1,650	£1,800	£2,00	£2,200

3. What was the average number of sales across all six employees?

A	B	C	D
10	9.5	11.5	14

ANSWERS TO PRACTICE TEST 1

Question 1

1. B = 60 miles

2. A = 38 minutes

3. D = 1 hour and 12 minutes

Question 2

1. D = 87 sq m

→ 7 × 14 = 98
→ 1 × 11 = 11
→ 98 – 11 = 87 square metres

2. B = 6 sq m

→ From question 1, we know that the total area of Park 1 is 87 square metres.
→ Now we need to work out the total area of Park 2 9 × 2 = 18
→ 5 × 15 = 75
→ 18 + 75 = 93
→ So the difference between Park 1 and Park 2 = 93 – 87 = 6 square metres

3. C = 48%

→ 93 + 87 = 180 square metres
→ 87 ÷ 180 × 100 = 48.333
→ To the nearest whole number = 48

Question 3

1. A = 20

→ We know that there are 70 items of confectionary. We also know that there are 3.5 times as many confectionary items compared to drinks. So the sum is 70 ÷ 3.5 = 20

2. B = 500

→ We know that 70 items are confectionary, which make up 14%. So 1% of the store's items is 70 ÷ 14 = 5
→ 5 × 100 gives you the total amount of items in the store, which is 500.

3. C = 410

→ Using our answer to the previous question, we now know that there are 500 items in the store.
→ There are 70 items of confectionary, and 20 drinks in the store. That means the number of savoury items in the store = 500 – 20 – 70 = 410

Question 4

1. C = 22 hours and 30 minutes

→ There are 15 classes on during the week. If each class takes 90 minutes:
→ 15 × 90 = 1,350 minutes
→ Converted into hours and minutes: 1,350 ÷ 60 = 22.5 (which is equivalent to 22 hours and 30 minutes)

2. D = 5:3

→ During the seven days, there are 5 swimming classes and 3 legs, bums and tums classes. In a ratio, this would be 5:3.

3. B = £64.97

→ £14.99 × 3 = £44.97
→ 8 × £2.50 = £20.00
→ £44.97 + £20.00 = £64.97

Question 5

1. B = Dave

→ You need to work out the total sales for each employee:
  → Tom = 9
  → Dave = 15
  → Mary = 9
  → Alicia = 10
  → Logan = 14
  → Millie = 12
→ Therefore, Dave will receive the Christmas bonus.

2. B = £1,800

→ 20% of £1,500 = 1,500 ÷ 100 × 120 = 1,800

3. C = 11.5

→ Using your answer to (part 1), you can add them all up, and then divide it by how many people there are.
→ 9 + 15 + 9 + 10 + 14 + 12 = 69
→ 69 ÷ 6 = 11.5

PRACTICE TEST 2

QUESTION 1

The following table lists the type of bonus each member of staff will receive if they reach a specific number of sales per hour they work. The table has not yet been completed. Staff work seven hour shifts. In order to answer the questions, you will need to complete the table.

TIME	10 sales	20 sales	30 sales	40 sales
1st hour	£23.50	£27.50	£35.95	£42.60
2nd hour	£20.00	£23.50	-	£36.35
3rd hour	£16.50	-	£25.55	-
4th hour	£13.00	£15.50	£20.35	-
5th hour	£9.50	-	£15.15	£17.60
6th hour	-	£7.50	£9.95	£11.35
7th hour	£2.50	£3.50	-	£5.10

1. If the table was complete, how much could a worker earn in bonuses if they reached 10 sales every hour of their 7-hour shift?

A	B	C	D
£99.50	£101	£91.00	£98.50

2. How much would a worker earn in bonuses if they reached 20 sales per hour for the first 4 hours of their shift, and 40 sales per hour for the remaining 3 hours of their shift?

A	B	C	D
£120.05	£112.10	£120.05	£121.10

3. How much would a worker earn in bonuses if they reached 10 sales during their first and last hour, 20 sales during the 2nd and 6th hours, 30 sales during the 3rd and 5th hours, and 40 sales during the 4th hour?

A	B	C	D
£124.50	£124	£125.55	£121.55

QUESTION 2

Katie and Harrison take a road trip. There are two parts of the journey so they decide to split the driving. For the first, Katie drives 90 miles at an average speed of 60 mph. They stop off at a petrol station for 20 minutes, before Harrison takes over the next part of the journey. They leave the petrol station at 1355 and arrive at their destination at 1525, travelling a distance of 60 miles.

1. How long does the first part of the journey take?

A	B	C	D
1 hour and 30 minutes	1 hour	2 hours	2 hours and 15 minutes

2. What is the duration of the whole journey, including the stop off?

A	B	C	D
4 hours	3 hours and 20 minutes	3 hours and 45 minutes	4 hours and 15 minutes

3. What speed do you travel at for the second part of the journey?

A	B	C	D
30 mph	35 mph	40 mph	45 mph

QUESTION 3

The pie chart below shows the percentage of students in each faculty at Grove University, and the number of Non-US students in the Business faculty. These percentages have been rounded to the nearest whole number.

There are a total of 1,247 students in the Business faculty.

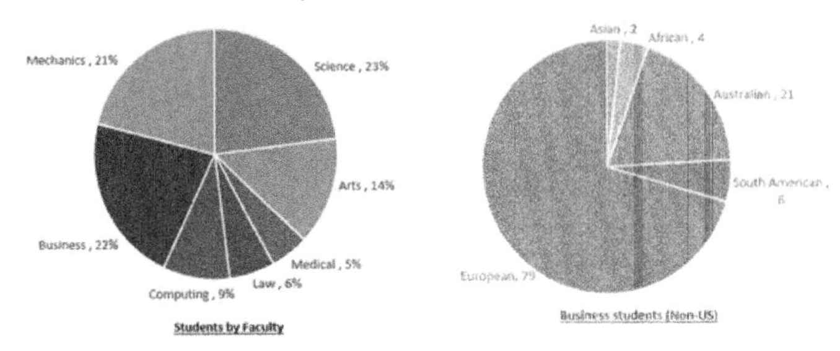

1. What percentage of students in the Business faculty are Non-US students?

A	B	C	D
11%	13%	9%	7%

2. How many students are there at the university?

A	B	C	D
5,558	5,668	5,685	55,85

3. How many students are there studying Law?

A	B	C	D
310	290	380	340

QUESTION 4

Below are the test scores of 24 people. The test was a General Knowledge quiz. The test is marked out of 100.

64	53	19	75	33	51
46	87	47	49	91	90
26	18	55	50	64	76
14	49	62	80	80	65

1. What was the combined total of marks for all 24 people?

A	B	C	D
1,344	1,434	1,334	1,444

2. What was the mean score across all of the results?

A	B	C	D
52	48	64	56

3. What percentage of the total number of people scored 50 or more in the General Knowledge quiz?

A	B	C	D
61.5%	50%	62.5%	60%

QUESTION 5

On Monday mornings, it is your duty to ensure all vehicles are fuelled and cleaned. There are 5 stops; you spend 20 minutes at each. Each stop is 7 miles apart. The first stop is 42 miles away, and you travel at a constant speed of 70 mph.

1. What time will you finish at the first stop, if you leave at 06:30?

A	B	C	D
07:32	07:18	07:10	07:26

2. Assuming you did not stop at any of the stops, and left your house at 06:30, what distance would you have travelled by 08:00?

A	B	C	D
152 miles	105 miles	160 miles	98 miles

3. Including the stops, how long will it take you to complete the whole journey?

A	B	C	D
1 hour and 30 minutes	2 hours and 50 minutes	2 hours and 40 minutes	1 hour and 50 minutes

ANSWERS TO PRACTICE TEST 2

Question 1

1. C = £91

→ £23.50 + £20.00 + £16.50 + £13.00 + £9.50 + £6.00 + £2.50 = £91.00

2. A = £120.05

→ £27.50 + £23.50 + £19.50 + £15.50 = £86

→ £17.60 + £11.35 + £5.10 = £34.05

→ £86.00 + £34.05 = £120.05

3. D = £121.55

→ £23.50 + £2.50 + £23.50 + £7.50 + £25.55 + £15.15 + £23.85 = £121.55

Question 2

1. A = 1 hour and 30 minutes

2. B = 3 hours and 20 minutes

3. C = 40 mph

Question 3

1. C = 9%

→ 112 ÷ 1,247 × 100 = 8.98. Rounded to the nearest whole number = 9%.

2. B = 5,668

→ 1,247 × 100 ÷ 22 = 5,668

3. D = 340

→ 5,668 ÷ 100 × 6 = 340

Question 4

1. A = 1,344

→ Add up all of the test scores = 1,344

2. D = 56

→ To work out the mean, add up all of the numbers, and then divide it by how many numbers there are.
→ 1344 ÷ 24 = 56

3. C = 62.5%

→ Out of the 24 people, 15 of them scored 50 or more marks in the test.
→ 15 ÷ 24 × 100 = 62.5%

Question 5

1. D = 07:26

→ 42 miles at 70 mph = 36 minutes.
→ If the stop takes 20 minutes, that means it's taken 56 minutes to get to the first stop and get the first stop done.
→ If you left at 06:30, that means you would finish the first stop at 07:26

2. B = 105 miles

3. C = 2 hours and 40 minutes

→ To get to the first stop, it takes you 36 minutes. Each stop you need to spend 20 minutes there.
→ There are 5 stops which will take 1 hour and 40 minutes.
→ To get to stop 1 to stop 2, stop 2 to stop 3, and so forth, takes 6 minutes.
→ That means it takes 24 minutes for each step. If you add up all of these, these works out to be 2 hours and 40 minutes.

PRACTICE TEST 3

QUESTION 1

Northshire Enterprises have put out a tender for electrical equipment and supplies. Below are quotes from 3 suppliers.

Electrical Equipment and supplies	Supplier 1 Total cost over 2 years (£)	Supplier 2 Total cost over 2 years (£)	Supplier 3 Total cost over 1 year (£)
Basic Services	34,550	36,660	15,450
Electrical safety Check	39,550	42,000	20,000
Full Equipment Maintenance	120,850	150,500	60,000

1. Based on an annual year cost, which supplier offers the best price for electrical safety checks?

A	B	C	D
Supplier 1	Supplier 2	Supplier 3	They are the same

2. What percentage of the total quote provided by supplier 1 accounts for basic services?

A	B	C	D
17%	17.7%	18.5%	18.3%

3. Based on 2 years, what supplier provides the cheapest quote overall for electrical equipment and supplies?

A	B	C	D
Supplier 1	Supplier 2	Supplier 3	Supplier 2 and 3

QUESTION 2.

Smith's Premium Properties have put out a tender for security checks and system updates. Below are quotes from 3 suppliers.

Security checks and system updates	Supplier 1 Total cost over 2 years (£)	Supplier 2 Total cost over 4 years (£)	Supplier 3 Total cost over 5 years (£)
Basic Security Check	26,330	40,560	52,550
Advanced Security Check	52,530	104,320	120,880
Updating software and security	15,430	31,220	32,000

1. What percentage of the total quote provided by Supplier 2 accounts for updating software and security?

A	B	C	D
12.4%	17.7%	19.2%	None of these

2. For the total cost over 5 years, what supplier provides the cheapest quote overall for security checks and system updates?

A	B	C	D
Supplier 1	Supplier 2	Supplier 3	Supplier 1 and 2

3. Based on an annual cost, what supplier provides the most expensive quote for basic security cost?

A	B	C	D
Supplier 1	Supplier 2	Supplier 3	All the same

QUESTION 3.

McDoogal's Marvellous Medicine have put out a tender for cleaning and support services. Below are quotes from 3 supplier.

Cleaning and support services	Supplier 1 Total cost over 2 years (£)	Supplier 2 Total cost over 3 years (£)	Supplier 3 Total cost over 4 years (£)
Basic cleaning services	15,050	19,850	22,500
Window cleaning	12,000	15,000	16,500
Specialist cleaning services	19,500	22,550	25,550

1. Which supplier, based on 1 year, provides the cheapest quote for window cleaning?

A	B	C	D
Supplier 1	Supplier 2	Supplier 3	All the same

2. Based on a 2 year cost, which supplier is the cheapest for specialist cleaning services?

A	B	C	D
Supplier 1	Supplier 2	Supplier 3	All the same

3. What percentage of the total quote provided by Supplier 3 accounts for basic cleaning services?

A	B	C	D
31.1%	32.5%	33.8%	34.9%

QUESTION 4.

Ficville Establishments have put out a tender for electrical services. Below are quotes from 3 suppliers.

Electrical Services	Supplier 1 Total cost over 4 years (£)	Supplier 2 Total cost over 2 years (£)	Supplier 3 Total cost over 2 years (£)
Fixed wire testing	16,500	10,250	11,000
Installations	21,050	12,500	16,400
Load analysis	28,000	17,000	16,000

1. Based on an annual one year cost, which supplier provides the cheapest load analysis service?

A	B	C	D
Supplier 1	Supplier 2	Supplier 3	All the same

2. For the total cost for 3 years, which supplier provides the most expensive quote overall for fixed wire testing?

A	B	C	D
Supplier 1	Supplier 2	Supplier 3	All the same

3. Based on an annual one year cost and everything the supplier has to offer, which supplier is the most expensive?

A	B	C	D
Supplier 1	Supplier 2	Supplier 3	All the same

QUESTION 5.

Sophie's Sparkling Footspas Ltd have put out a tender for a charity event in order to raise money for their chosen charity every year. Below are quotes from 3 suppliers.

Charity event	Supplier 1 Total cost over 1 year (£)	Supplier 2 Total cost over 3 years (£)	Supplier 3 Total cost over 4 years (£)
Disco / Party	13,000	29,350	43,500
Fun fair	11,500	33,050	38,800
Outdoors assault course	12,000	35,800	40,500

1. Based on an annual one year cost, which supplier provides the cheapest overall quote for a disco/party charity event?

A	B	C	D
Supplier 1	Supplier 2	Supplier 3	All the same

2. What percentage of the total quote provided by Supplier 3 accounts for outdoors assault course?

A	B	C	D
32.9%	33%	34%	33.3%

3. Based on an annual year, what is the average cost that suppliers charge for hosting a fun fair? Rounded to the nearest whole number.

A	B	C	D
10,750	10,738	10,730	10,739

ANSWERS TO PRACTICE TEST 3

Question 1

1. Supplier 1

→ Work out which of the suppliers has the cheapest electrical safety checks by working out the cost per year for each supplier.

→ Supplier 1's cost is based over two years so divide the cost by 2 to find out the annual cost which is £19,775 per year.

→ Supplier 2's cost is also based over two years, so divided by two the annual cost is, £21,000.

→ The cost for Supplier 3 is £20,000, so the cheapest quote from the three is Supplier 1, £19,775.

2. 17.7%

→ Work out the percentage costs for Basic Services by adding the 3 amounts together, £34,550 + £39,550 + £120,850 = £194,950 total cost.

→ £34,550 ÷ £194,950 x 100 = 17.72

→ Rounded to 17.7.

3. Supplier 3

→ Add Supplier 3's costs together and multiply by two.

→ £15,450 + £20,000 + £60,000 = £95,450 × 2 = £190,900, which is cheaper than both Suppliers 1, £194950 and Supplier 2 £229160.

Question 2

1. 17.7%

→ Work out the percentage costs for Updating Software and Security of Supplier 2 by adding the 3 prices together.

→ £40,560 + £104,320 + £31,220 = £176,100.

→ Then £31,220 ÷ £176,100 × 100 = 17.72.

→ Rounded to 17.7.

2. Supplier 3

- → Find the annual cost for each supplier by dividing the number of years the quote is based on by the cost of all services combined.
- → Supplier 1; £26,330 + £52,530 + £15,430 = £94,290. As the quotation is based on 2 years, divide £94,290 by 2 to get the annual cost of £47,145.
- → Work out the cost over 5 years by multiplying the annual cost by 5; £47,145 × 5 = £235,725.
- → Supplier 2; £40,560 + £104,320 + £31,220 = £176,100 over 4 years.
- → £176,100 ÷ 4 = £44,025. Then multiply by 5 = £220,125.
- → Supplier 3; £52,550 + £120,880 + £32,000 = £205,430.
- → Supplier 3's quote is already based on 5 years no further calculations are required.
- → Supplier 3 has the cheapest quote over 5 years £205,430.

3. Supplier 1

- → Supplier 1; The total cost for Basic Security checks is based on two years, so divide this by 2.
- → £26,330 ÷ 2 = £13,165.
- → Supplier 2; £40,560 over 4 years, divide this by 4 for annual cost.
- → £40,560 ÷ 4 = £10,140.
- → Supplier 3; £52,550 over 5 years, divide this by 5 for annual cost.
- → £52,550 ÷ 5 = £10,510.

Question 3

1. Supplier 3

- → Supplier 1. Divide 12,000 by 2 to get annual cost of 6,000.
- → Supplier 2. Divide 15,000 by 3 to get annual cost of 5,000.
- → Supplier 3. Divide 16,500 by 4 to get annual cost of 4,125.

2. Supplier 3

→ Supplier 1; No calculations required as the quote is already based on 2 years, which is £19,500.

→ Supplier 2; As the quote is based over 3 years calculate £22,550 ÷ 3 = £7,517 (rounded up) then multiply by 2.

→ £7,517 × 2 = £15,034.

→ Supplier 3; This quote is based over 4 years so, £25,550 ÷ 2 = £12,775.

3. 34.9%

→ Work out the percentage costs for Basic Cleaning Services of Supplier 3 by adding the 3 prices together.

→ £22,500 + £16,500 + £25,550 = £64,550.

→ To find out the percentage cost: £22,500 / £64,550 × 100 = 34.85.

→ Rounded to 34.9.

Question 4

1. Supplier 1

→ Supplier 1; 28,000 ÷ 4 = 7,000.

→ Supplier 2; 17,000 ÷ 2 = 8,500.

→ Supplier 3; 16,000 ÷ 2 = 8,000.

2. Supplier 3

→ Supplier 1; 16,500 ÷ 4 = 4,125 × 3 = 12,375.

→ Supplier 2; 10,250 ÷ 2 = 5,125 × 3 = 15,375.

→ Supplier 3; 11,000 ÷ 2 = 5,500 × 3 = 16,500.

3. Supplier 3

→ Supplier 1; 16,500 + 21,050 + 28,000 = 65,550 ÷ 4 = 16,387.50.

→ Supplier 2; 10,250 + 12,500 + 17,000 = 39,750 ÷ 2 = 19,875.

→ Supplier 3; 11,000 + 16,400 + 16,000 = 43,400 ÷ 2 = 21,700.

Question 5

1. Supplier 2

→ Work this out by calculating each suppliers annual cost.

→ Supplier 1; No calculation required as the quote is already based on 1 year. £13,000.

→ Supplier 2; £29,350 ÷ 3 = £9,783.

→ Supplier 3; £43,500 ÷ 4 = £10,875.

2. 33%

→ To work out the percentage costs for full system and computer check and updates of Supplier 3, add the 3 amounts together.

→ £43,500 + £38,800 + £40,500 = £122,800.

→ Then do the following calculation to find out the percentage cost. £40,500 ÷ £122,800 x 100 = 32.98.

→ Rounded to 33%.

3. £10,739

→ Work out the average annual cost of all suppliers combined by ascertaining the annual cost for each supplier for hosting a fun fair.

→ Supplier 1; The quote is based on 1 year £11,500.

→ Supplier 2; £33,050 ÷ 3 = £11,017.

→ Supplier 3; £38,800 ÷ 4 = £9,700.

→ Then add the totals together and divide by the number of values, in this case 3.

→ £8,025 + £11,500 + £11,016 + £9,700 = £23,100 ÷ 3 = £7,700.

ABSTRACT REASONING

Abstract Reasoning tests measure your ability to identify patterns and relationships in shapes. These can come in a number of different forms, whether it's identifying the missing shape in the sequence, spotting the odd one out, or pairing similar shapes together. This is possibly the hardest part of the assessment, and the area that most candidates fall down on, so it's important to undergo significant revision prior to taking the test.

Have a go at the questions below, and see how you get on. The answer to every question has been explained following the test.

PRACTICE TEST 1

Q1. The middle row of boxes create a rule that has been applied to the boxes directly above them. Which answer option (A to E) corresponds to the rule under the box with the question mark?

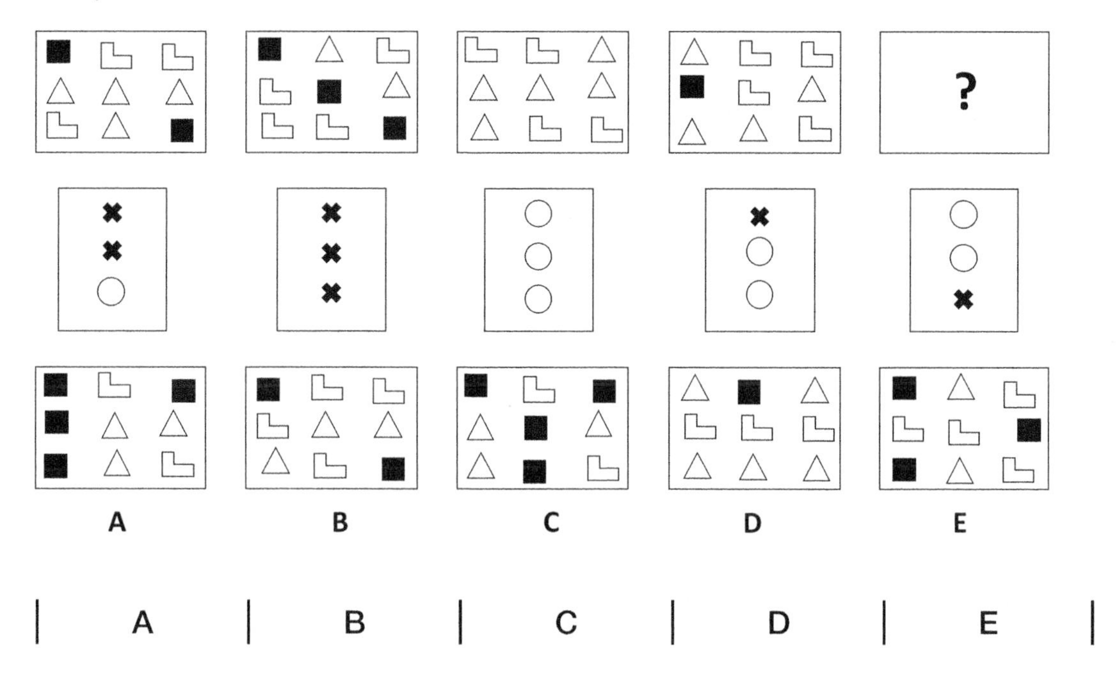

A	B	C	D	E

Q2. The middle row of boxes create a rule that has been applied to the boxes directly above them. Which answer option (A to E) corresponds to the rule under the box with the question mark?

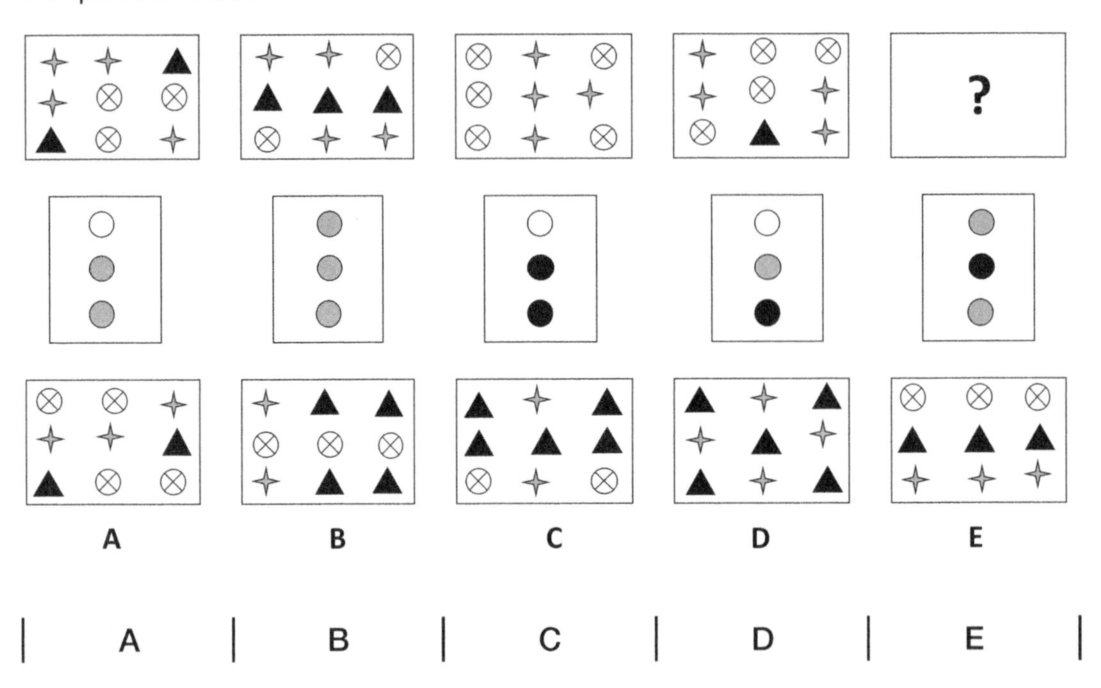

Q3. The middle row of boxes create a rule that has been applied to the boxes directly above them. Which answer option (A to E) corresponds to the rule under the box with the question mark?

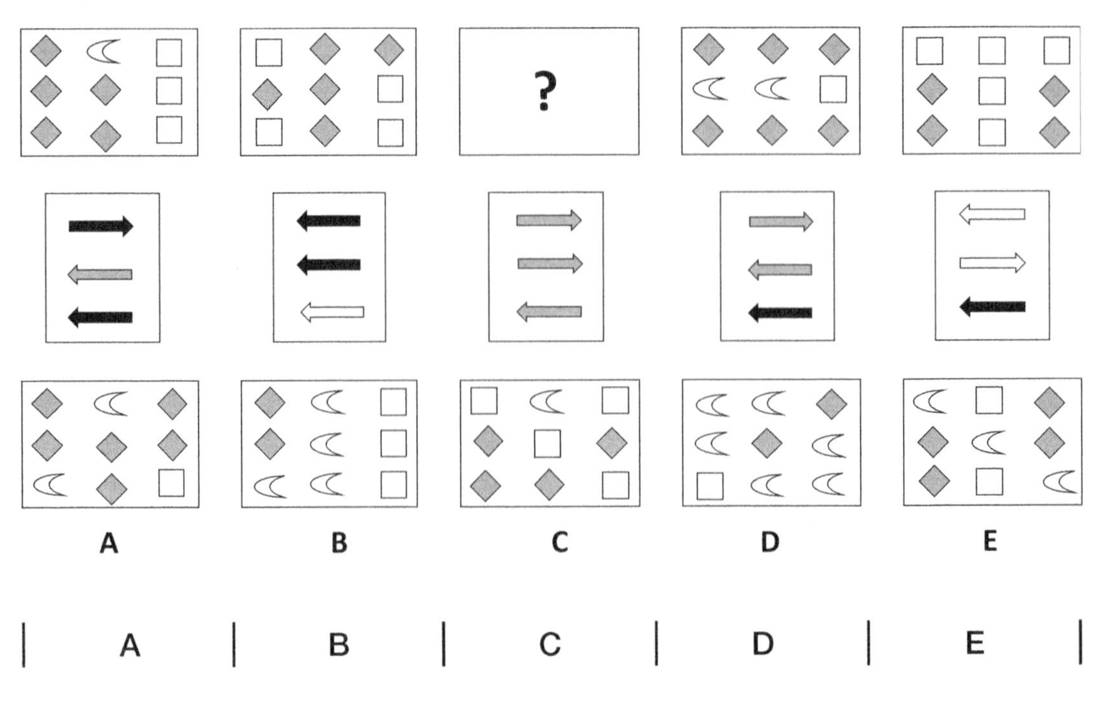

Q4. The middle row of boxes create a rule that has been applied to the boxes directly above them. Which answer option (A to E) corresponds to the rule under the box with the question mark?

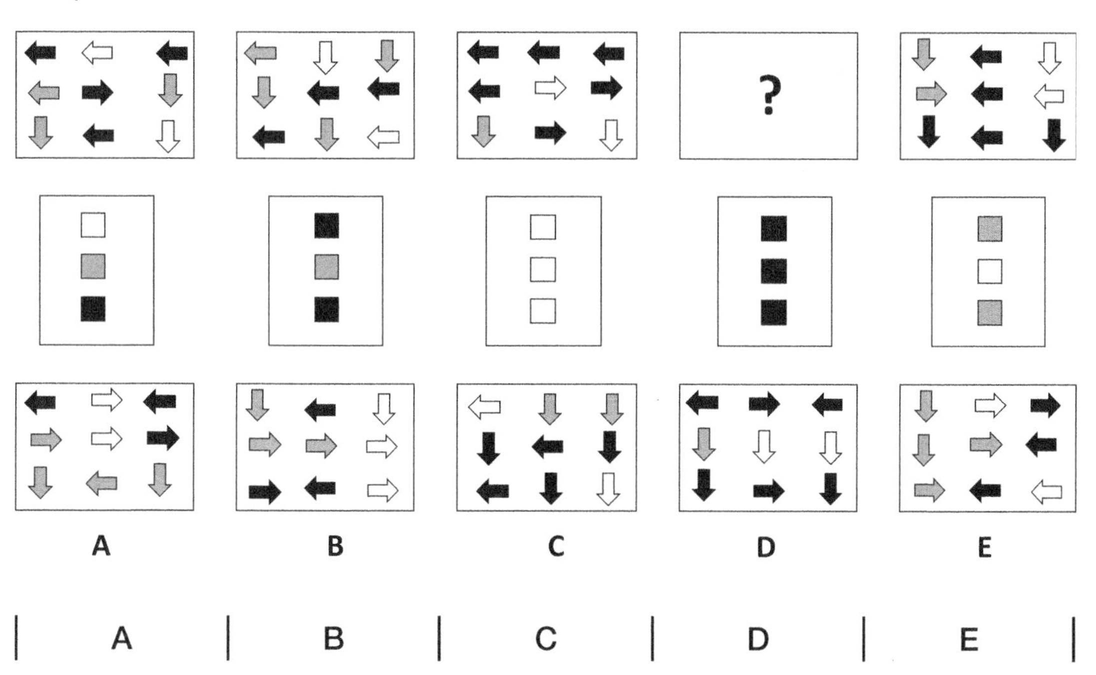

Q5. The middle row of boxes create a rule that has been applied to the boxes directly above them. Which answer option (A to E) corresponds to the rule under the box with the question mark?

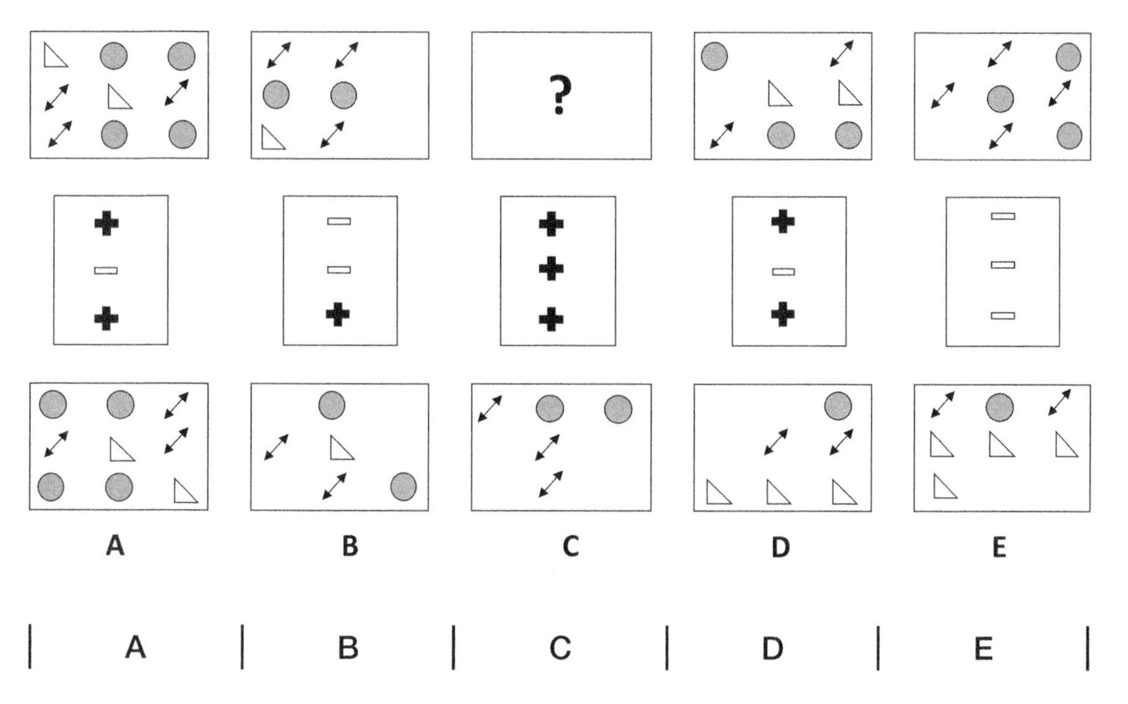

Q6. The middle row of boxes create a rule that has been applied to the boxes directly above them. Which answer option (A to E) corresponds to the rule under the box with the question mark?

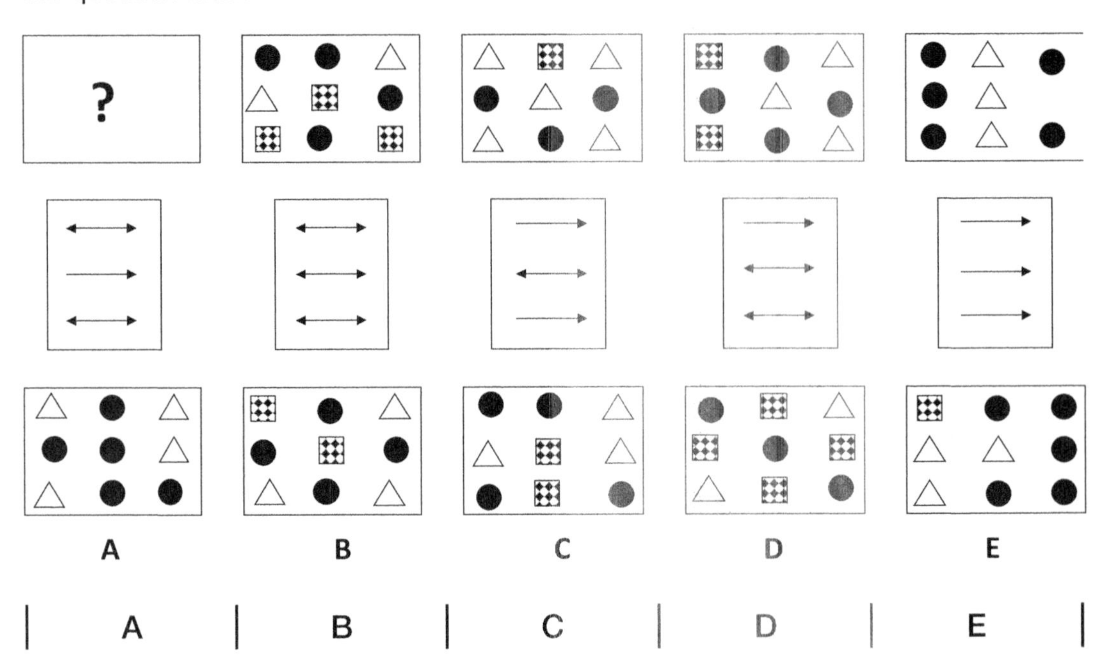

A	B	C	D	E

Q7. The middle row of boxes create a rule that has been applied to the boxes directly above them. Which answer option (A to E) corresponds to the rule under the box with the question mark?

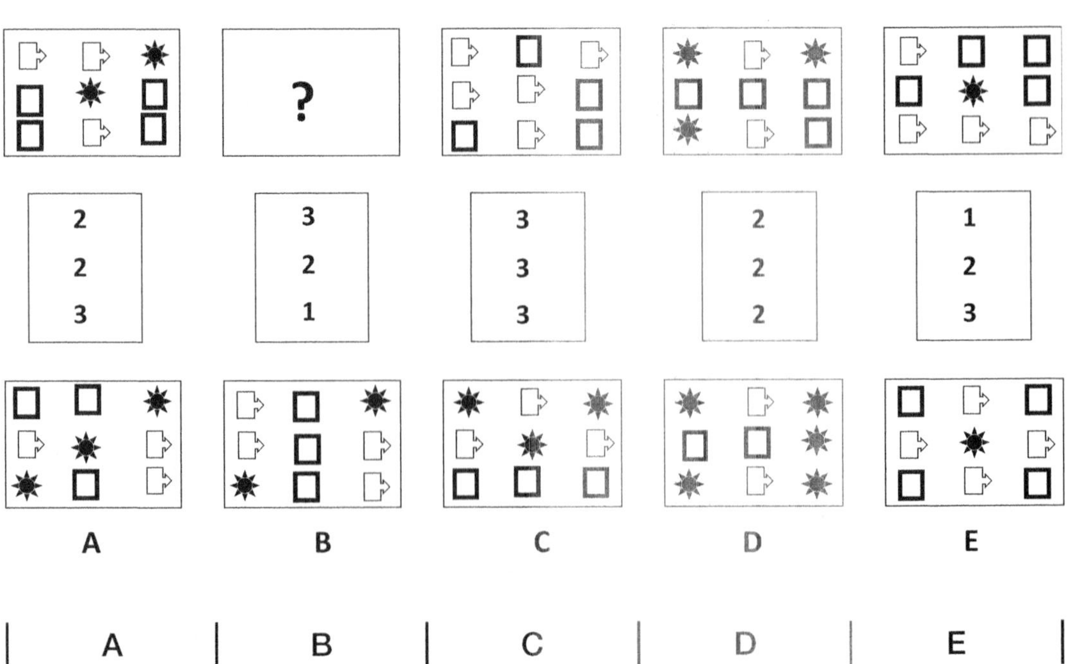

A	B	C	D	E

Q8. The middle row of boxes create a rule that has been applied to the boxes directly above them. Which answer option (A to E) corresponds to the rule under the box with the question mark?

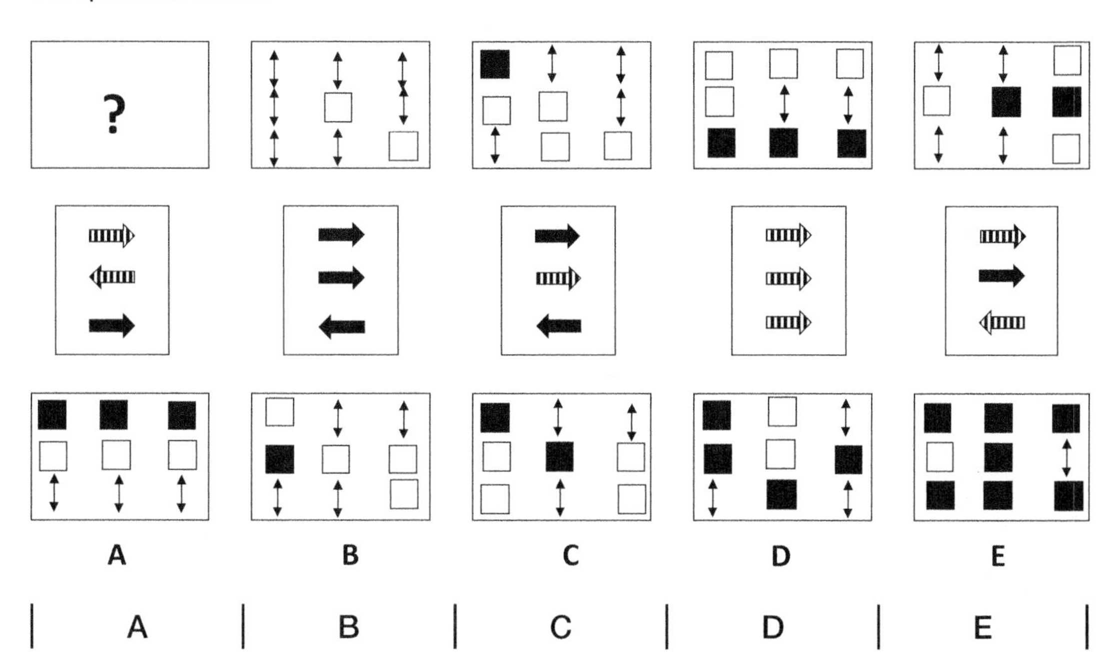

A	B	C	D	E

Q9. The middle row of boxes create a rule that has been applied to the boxes directly above them. Which answer option (A to E) corresponds to the rule under the box with the question mark?

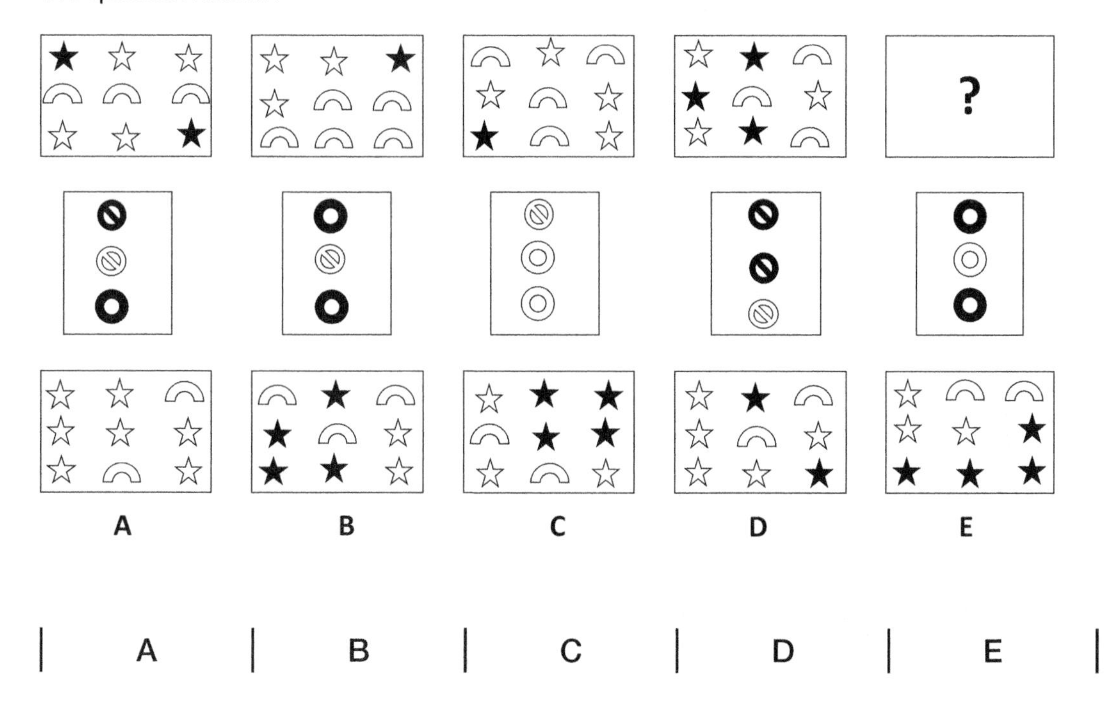

A	B	C	D	E

Q10. The middle row of boxes create a rule that has been applied to the boxes directly above them. Which answer option (A to E) corresponds to the rule under the box with the question mark?

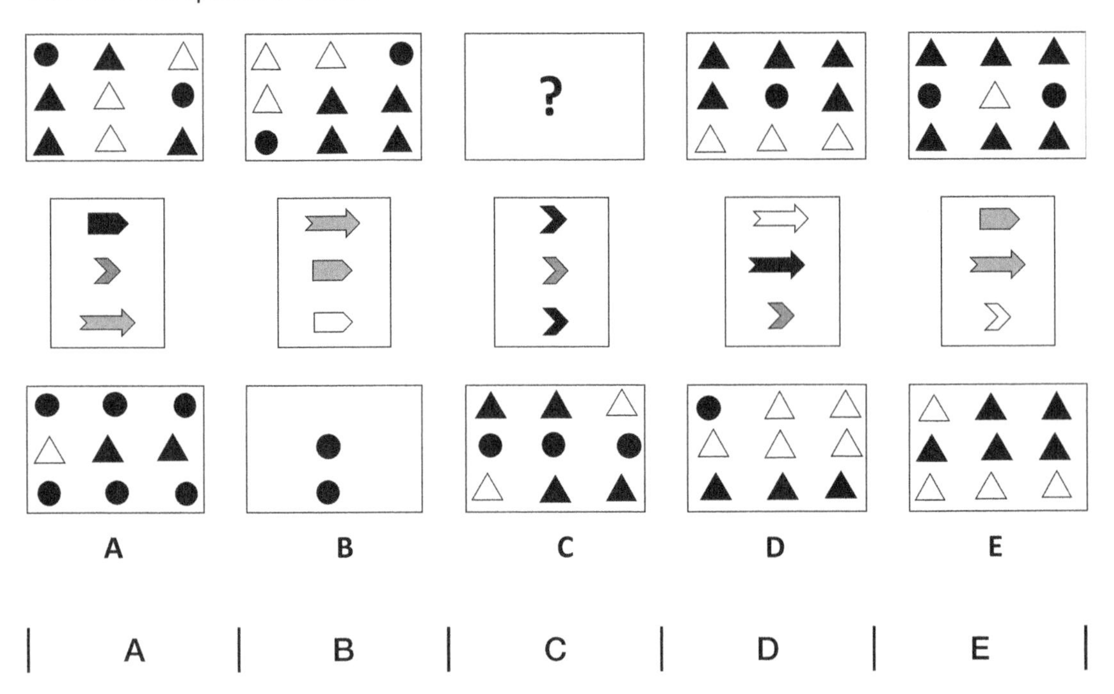

A	B	C	D	E

ANSWERS TO PRACTICE TEST 1

Q1. D

The rule in this question sees the black crosses dictating the number of squares in the pattern above. The rule being applied to box with the question mark means that only one black square should appear in the answer.

Q2. A

The rule in this question sees the grey circles dictating the number of black triangles in the pattern above. The rule being applied to box with the question mark means that two black triangles should appear in the answer.

Q3. E

The rule in this question sees the grey arrows dictating the number of moon shapes in the pattern above. The rule being applied to box with the question mark means that three moon shapes should appear in the answer.

Q4. C

The rule in this question sees the white square dictating the number of arrows pointing to the right in the pattern above. The rule being applied to box with the question mark means that no arrows pointing to the right should appear in the answer.

Q5. D

The rule in this question sees the black plus signs dictating the triangles in the pattern above. The rule being applied to box with the question mark means that three triangles should appear in the answer.

Q6. B

The rule in this question sees the double-sided arrow dictating the number of patterned squares in the pattern above. The rule being applied to box with the question mark means that two patterned squares should appear in the answer.

Q7. E

The rule in this question sees the number '2' dictating the number of sun shapes in the pattern above. The rule being applied to box with the question mark means that one sun shape should appear in the answer.

Q8. C

The rule in this question sees the number of patterned arrows dictating the number of black squares in the pattern above. The rule being applied to box with the question mark means that two black squares should appear in the answer.

Q9. A

The rule in this question sees the number of "not allowed" symbols dictating the number of black stars in the pattern above. The rule being applied to box with the question mark means that no "not allowed" symbols should appear in the answer.

Q10. D

The rule in this question sees the number grey shapes dictating the number of black circles in the pattern above. The rule being applied to box with the question mark means that one shape should appear in the answer.

PRACTICE TEST 2

Q1. Which SET does the TEST SHAPE belong to?

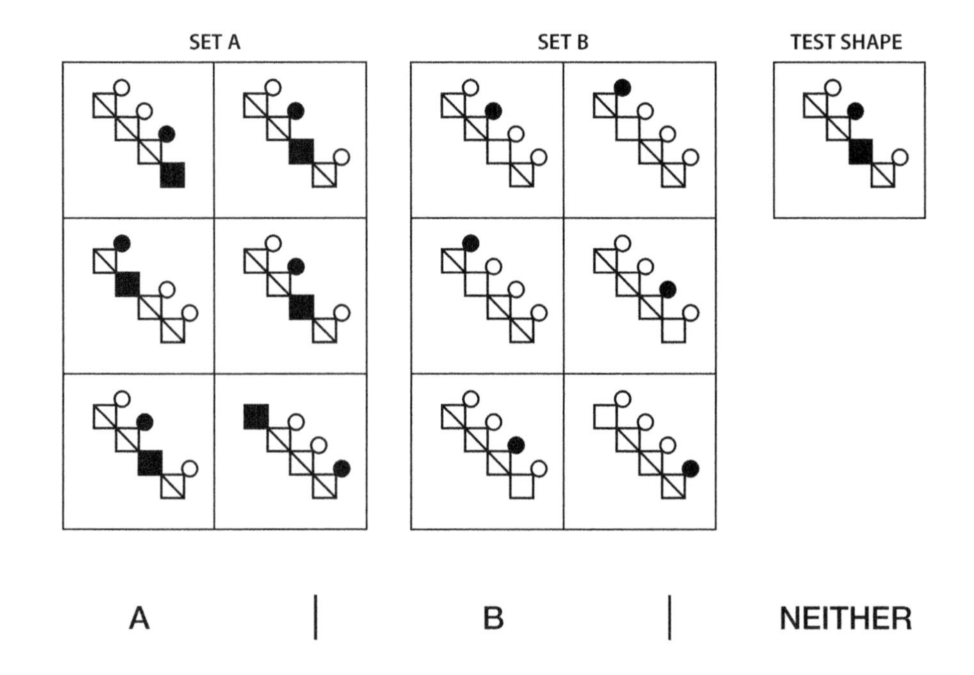

A	B	NEITHER

Q2. Which SET does the TEST SHAPE belong to?

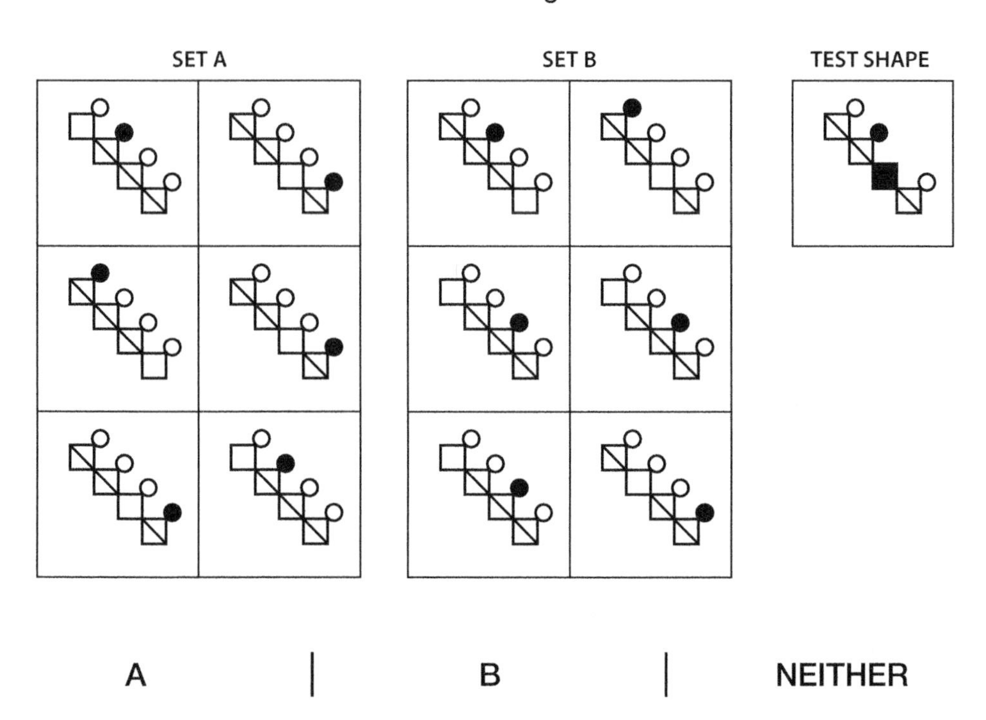

A	B	NEITHER

Q3. Which SET does the TEST SHAPE belong to?

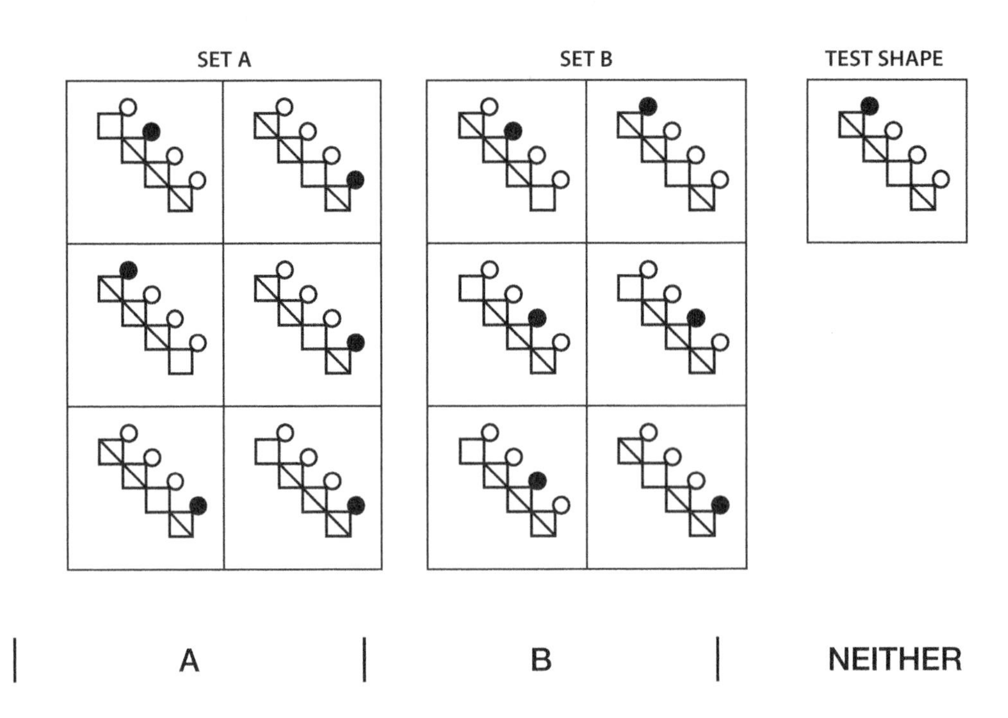

A	B	NEITHER

Q4. Which SET does the TEST SHAPE belong to?

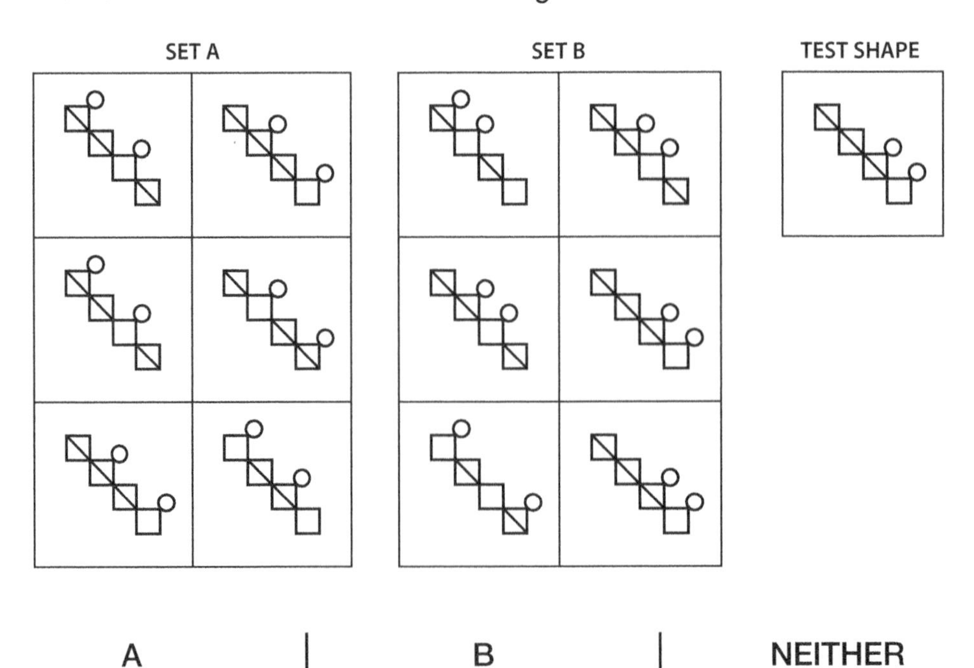

A	B	NEITHER

Q5. Which SET does the TEST SHAPE belong to?

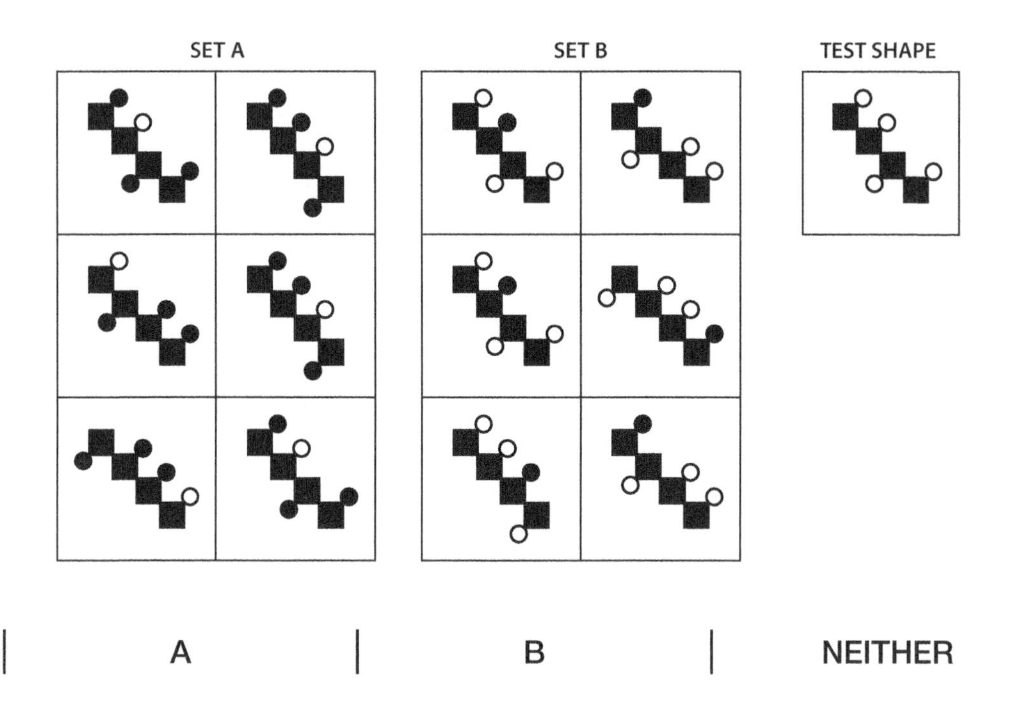

A	B	NEITHER

Q6. Which SET does the TEST SHAPE belong to?

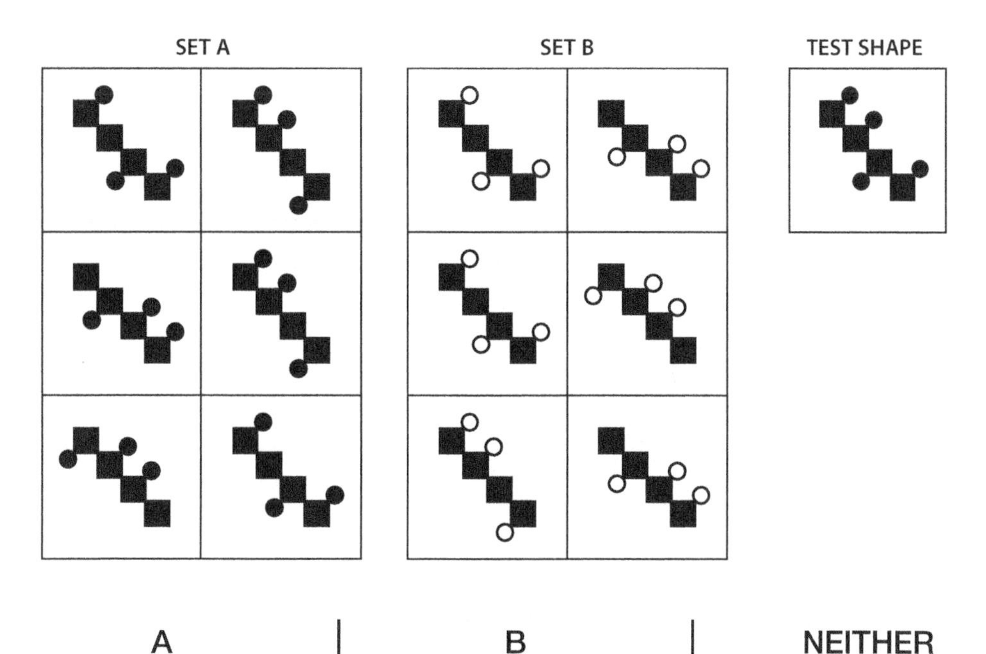

A	B	NEITHER

Q7. Which SET does the TEST SHAPE belong to?

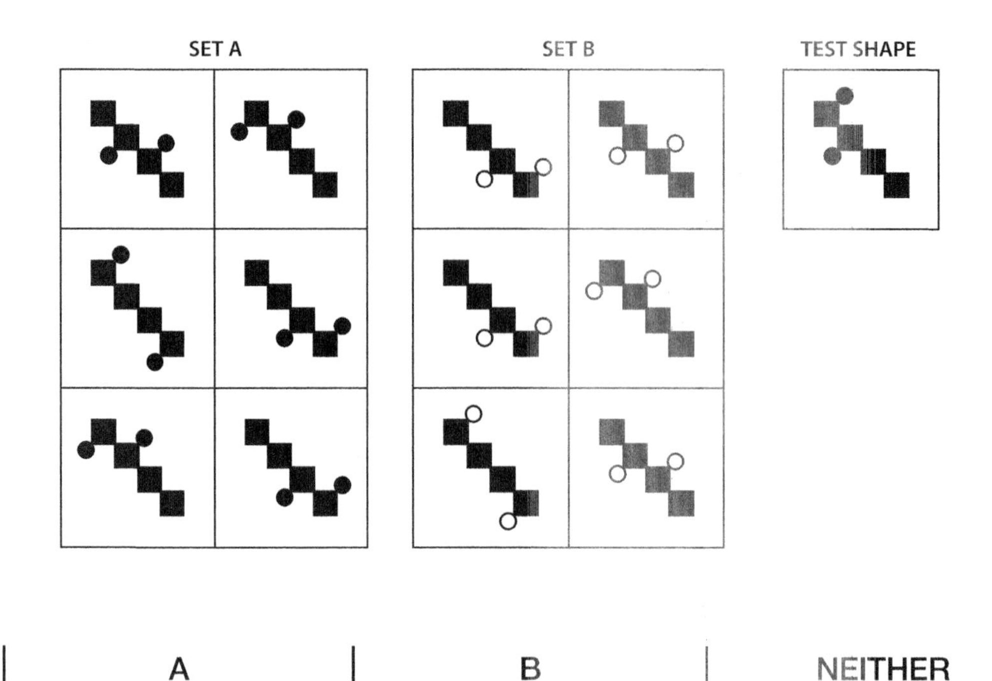

A	B	NEITHER

Q8. Which SET does the TEST SHAPE belong to?

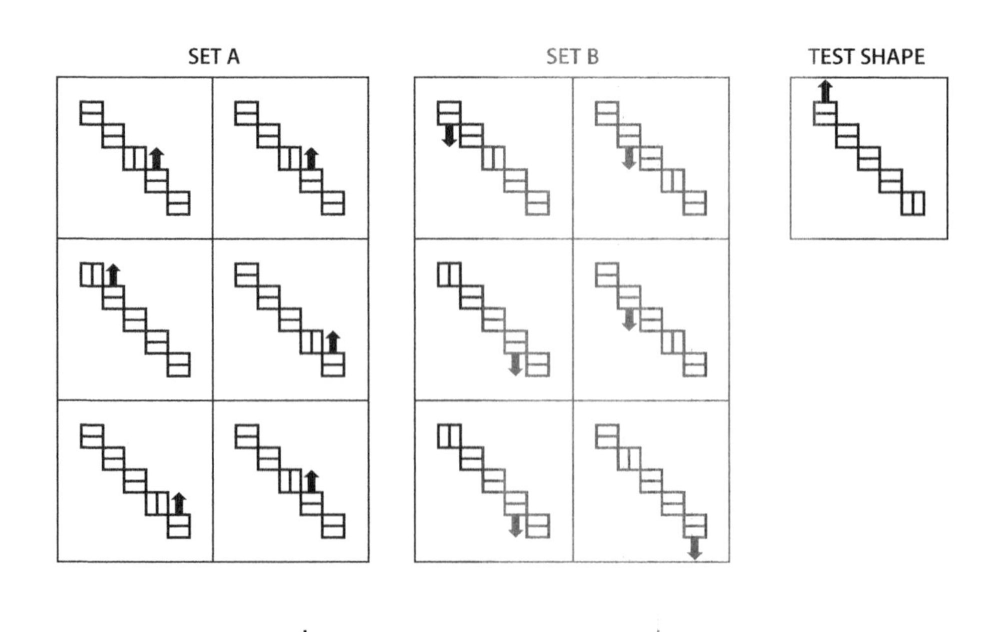

A	B	NEITHER

Q9. Which SET does the TEST SHAPE belong to?

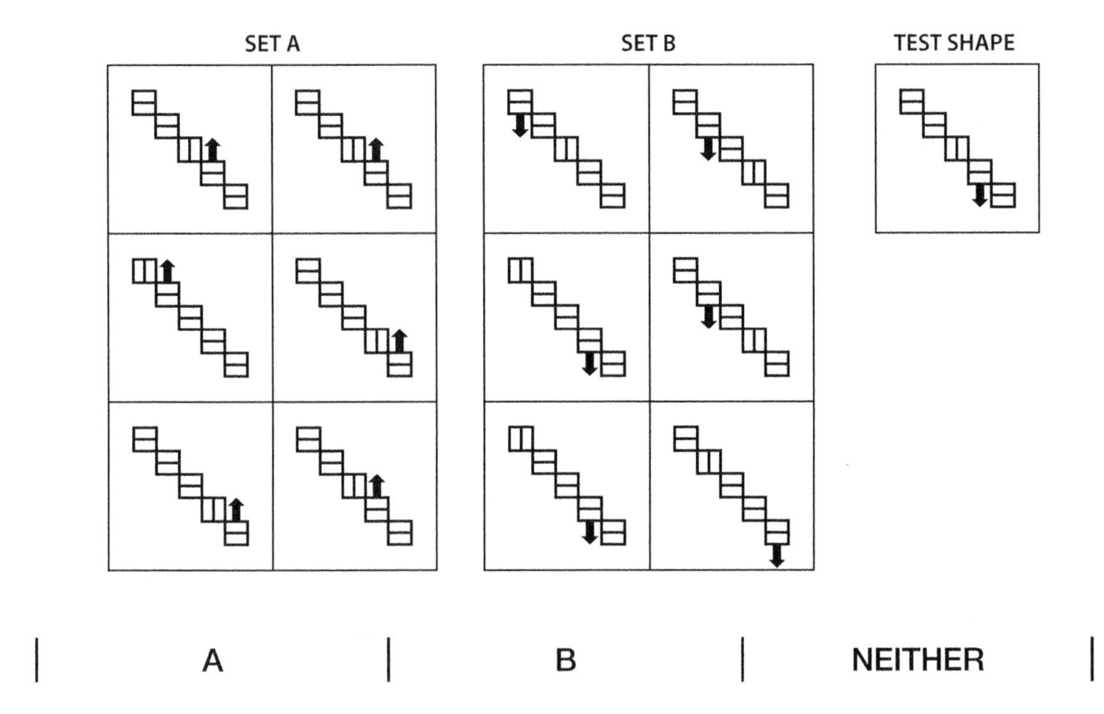

A	B	NEITHER

Q10. Which SET does the TEST SHAPE belong to?

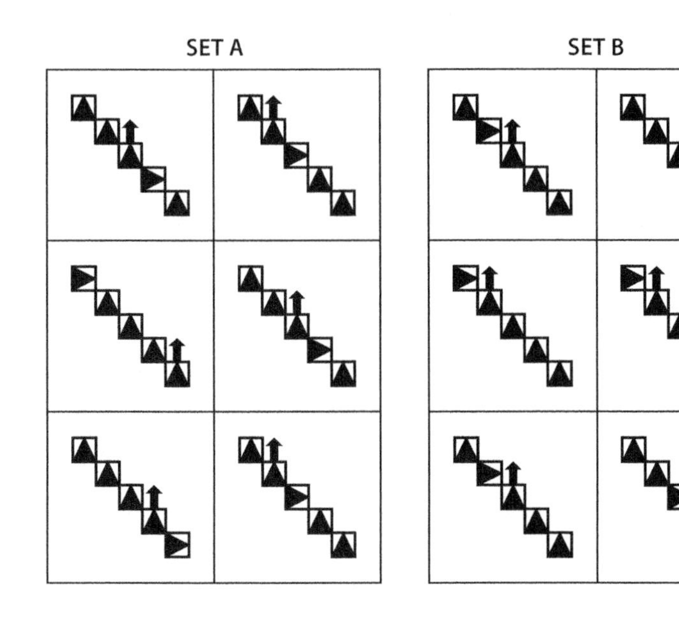

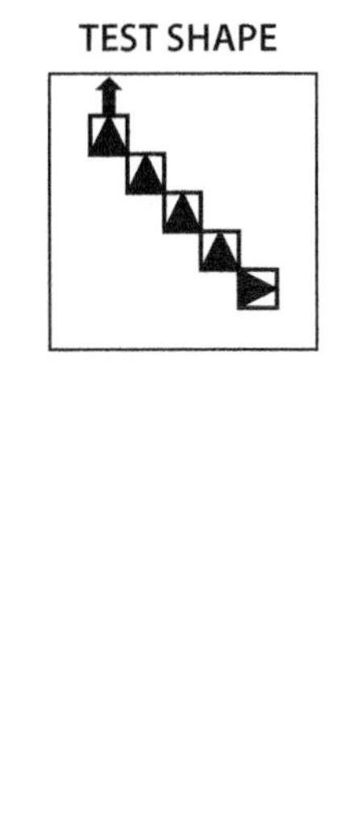

A	B	NEITHER

ANSWERS TO PRACTICE TEST 2

Q1. SET A

The Test Shape fits into Set A because it has two white dots and one black dot. It also has a black square and three squares with diagonal lines through them.

SET A: There are four squares, connected diagonally. Three of these squares are white, with a single diagonal line running through them, and one square is black. Three of these squares has a dot connected to them on their top right-hand corner. Two of the dots are white, whilst one is black. The dot on the square to the left of the black square is always black.

SET B: There are four squares, connected diagonally. All of the squares are white, and three of them have a diagonal line running through them. Each square has a dot connected to its top right-hand corner. Three of these dots are white, and one is black. The black dot is always connected to the square which is left of the square with no diagonal line running through it.

Q2. NEITHER

The Test Shape fits into neither of the two sets. Neither set contains a black square and the Test Shape does. Therefore, it doesn't belong to either set.

SET A: There are four squares in a diagonal line. If a square has no line running through it, then the next square down has a black dot. If the last square in the sequence of four has no line running through it then the first square will have a black dot.

SET B: There are four squares in a diagonal line. If a square has no line running through it, then the second square down from it will have a black dot. If the last square in the sequence of four has no line running through it then the second square from the top will have a black dot.

Q3. SET B

The Test Shape fits Set B because the black dot is two spaces down from the square that has no line running through it. This follows the pattern of Set B.

SET A: There are four squares in a diagonal line. If a square has no line running through it, then the next square down has a black dot. If the last square in the sequence of four has no line running through it then the first square will have a black dot.

SET B: There are four squares in a diagonal line. If a square has no line running through it then, the second square down from it will have a black dot. If the second from last square in the sequence of four has no line running through it, then the first square from the top will have a black dot.

Q4. SET B

The Test Shape fits with Set B because if the square has a diagonal line running through it and a white dot, the next square will have a white dot but no diagonal line in the square. The test shape follows this pattern.

SET A: There are four squares in a diagonal line. If a square has a line running through it and a white dot, then second square down from it also has a white dot but no line running through it. If the last square in the sequence of four is the one with a line running through it and a white dot, then the second square from the top with have a dot but no line running through it.

SET B: There are four squares in a diagonal line. If a square has a line running through it and a white dot then the next one down from it also has a white dot but no line running through it. If the last square in the sequence of four is the one with a line running through it and a white dot, then the first square at the top will have a dot but no line running through it.

Q5. NEITHER

The Test Shape doesn't fit in to either set. In Set A contains three black dots and only one white. Set B contains three white dots and only one black. The Test Shape has four white dots, so therefore cannot fit in to either set.

SET A: There are four black squares in a diagonal line. If a square has a white dot located in the top right-hand corner, then the next square down from it will have a black dot on the bottom left-hand corner. If the last square in the sequence of four is the one with a white dot, then the first square at the top of the sequence will be the one with a black dot on the bottom left-hand corner.

SET B: There are four black squares in a diagonal line. If a square has a black dot located in the top right-hand corner, then the next square down from it will have a white dot on the bottom left-hand corner. If the last square in the sequence of four is the one with a black dot, then the first square at the top of the sequence will be the one with a white dot on the bottom left-hand corner.

Q6. NEITHER

The Test Shape doesn't fit in to either set. In Set A, it contains three black dots. In Set B, it contains three white dots. The Test Shape contains four black dots and therefore cannot fit in to either set.

SET A: There are four black squares in a diagonal line. If a square has no dot located on the top right-hand corner, then the next square down from it will have a black dot on the bottom left-hand corner. If the last square in the sequence of four is the one with no dot, then the first square at the top of the sequence will be the one with a black dot on the bottom left-hand corner.

SET B: There are four black squares in a diagonal line. If a square has no dot located on the top right-hand corner, then the next square down from it will have a white dot on the bottom left-hand corner. If the last square in the sequence of four is the one with no dot, then the first square at the top of the sequence will be the one with a white dot on the bottom left-hand corner.

Q7. NEITHER

The Test Shape doesn't fit in to either set. In Set A, if a shaded square has a dot on the bottom left corner, then the next shaded square will have a dot on the top right corner. In Set B, the same thing is happening as seen in Set A, except they are white dots instead of black. The Test shape shows if the square has a dot on the top right corner, then the next square will have a dot on the bottom left corner.

SET A: There are four black squares in a diagonal line. If a square has a black dot located on the bottom left-hand corner, then the next square down from it will have a black dot on the top right-hand corner. If the last square in the sequence of four is the one with a black dot on the bottom left-hand corner, then the first square at the top of the sequence will be the one with a black dot on the right-hand corner.

SET B: There are four black squares in a diagonal line. If a square has a white dot located on the bottom left-hand corner, then the next square down from it will have a white dot on the top right-hand corner. If the last square in the sequence of four is the one with a white dot in the bottom left-hand corner, then the first square at the top of the sequence will be the one with a white dot in the right-hand corner.

Q8. SET A

The Test Shape fits with Set A. The first vertical square in the sequence means the next square will have an arrow pointing upwards. In the Test Shape, the vertical square is the last in the sequence, so the arrow will be placed at the start of the sequence.

SET A: There are five white squares in a diagonal line. If a square has a vertical line running through it then the next square will have a black arrow pointing upwards. If the last square in the sequence of five is the one with a vertical line running though it then the first square at the top of the sequence will be the one with an arrow pointing upwards.

SET B: There are five white squares in a diagonal line. If a square has an arrow pointing downwards then the second square that follows in the sequence will have a vertical line running through it. If the second to last square in the sequence of five is the one with an arrow pointing downwards then the first square at the top of the sequence will be the one with a vertical line running through it.

Q9. NEITHER

The Test Shapes doesn't fit in to either set. It cannot fit in to Set A because the arrows are pointing up and in the Test Shape, they are pointing down. In Set B, there are four consecutive squares that have horizontal lines, the arrow is placed on the third square. However, the Test Shape places the arrow on the first square that has a horizontal line.

SET A: There are five white squares in a diagonal line. If a square has a vertical line running through it then the next square will have a black arrow pointing upwards. If the last square in the sequence of five is the one with a vertical line running though it then the first square at the top of the sequence will be the one with an arrow pointing upwards.

SET B: There are five white squares in a diagonal line. If a square has an arrow pointing downwards then the second square that follows in the sequence will have a vertical line running through it. If the second to last square in the sequence of five is the one with an arrow pointing downwards then the first square at the top of the sequence will be the one with a vertical line running through it.

Q10. SET B

The Test Shape fits with Set B. If the triangle in the square is pointing to the right, then the next square will have an arrow pointing upwards. It cannot fit into Set A because the arrow is placed above the square that has the triangle pointing to the right.

SET A: There are five white squares in a diagonal line. If a square has an arrow standing on top of it, then the next square in the sequence will have a triangle pointing to the right inside it. If the last square in the sequence of five has an arrow standing on top of it, then the first square in the sequence will be the one with a triangle pointing to the right inside it.

SET B: There are five white squares in a diagonal line. If a square has a triangle pointing to the right inside it, then the next square in the sequence will have an arrow standing on top of it. If the last square in the sequence of five is the one a triangle pointing to the right inside it, then the first square in the sequence will be the one with an arrow standing on top of it.

PRACTICE TEST 3

Q1. Which figure comes next in the series?

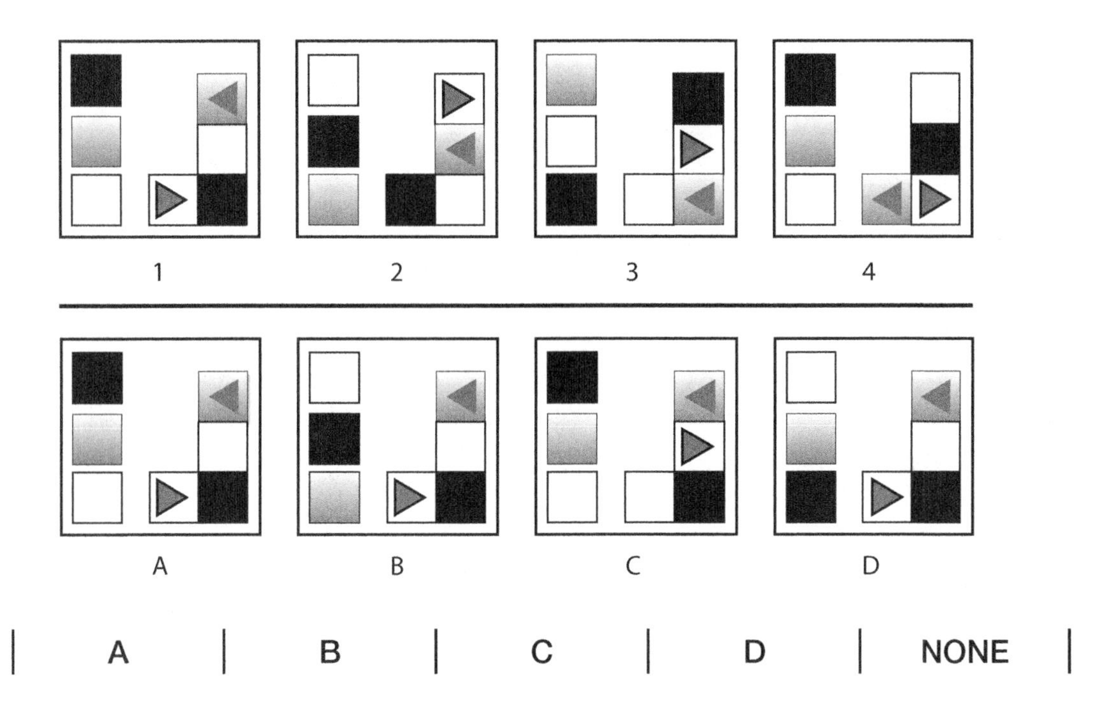

| A | B | C | D | NONE |

Q2. Which figure comes next in the series?

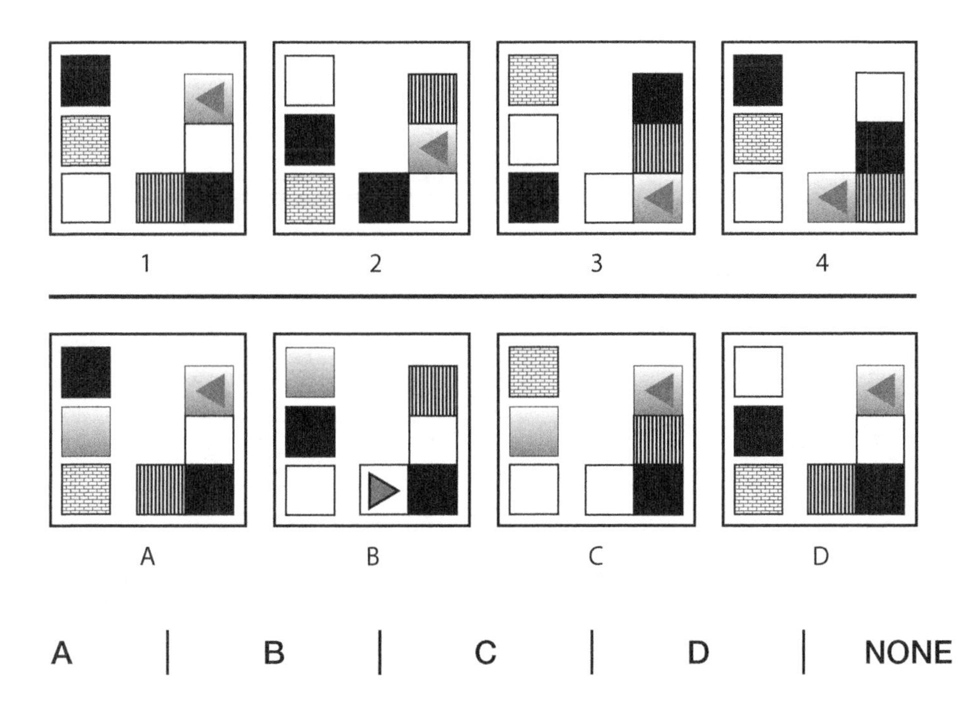

| A | B | C | D | NONE |

Q3. Which figure comes next in the series?

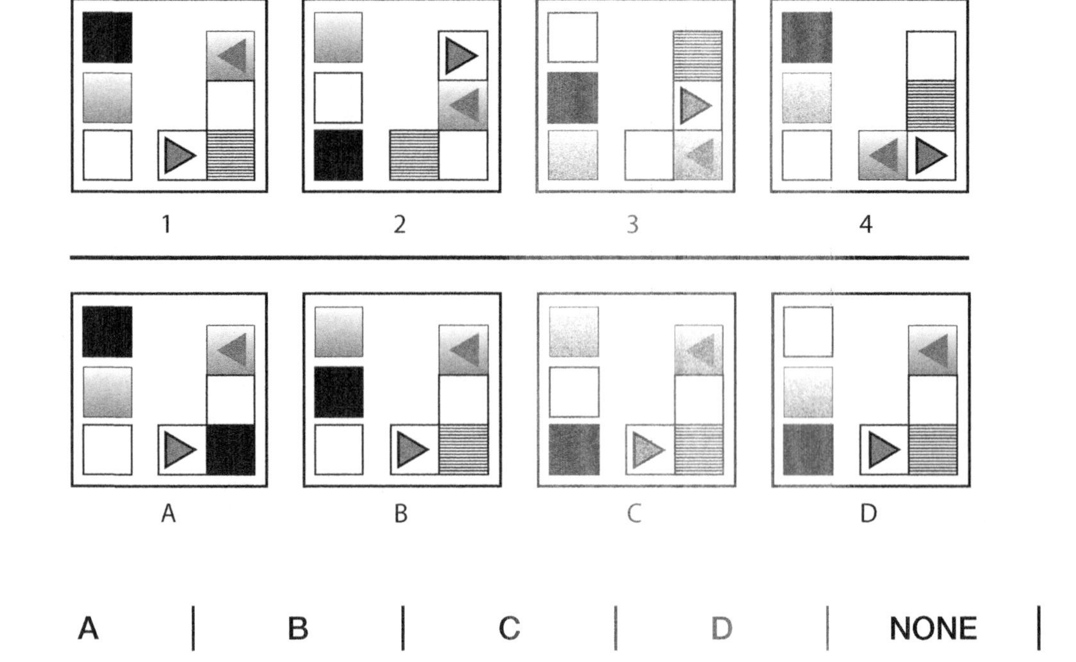

| A | B | C | D | NONE |

Q4. Which figure comes next in the series?

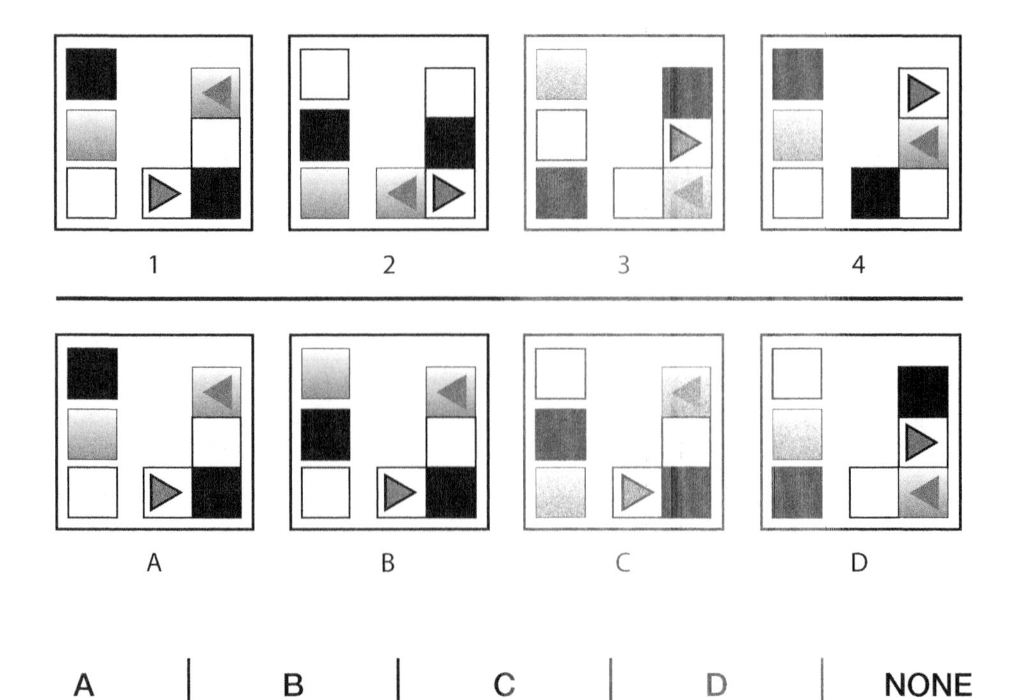

| A | B | C | D | NONE |

Q5. Which figure comes next in the series?

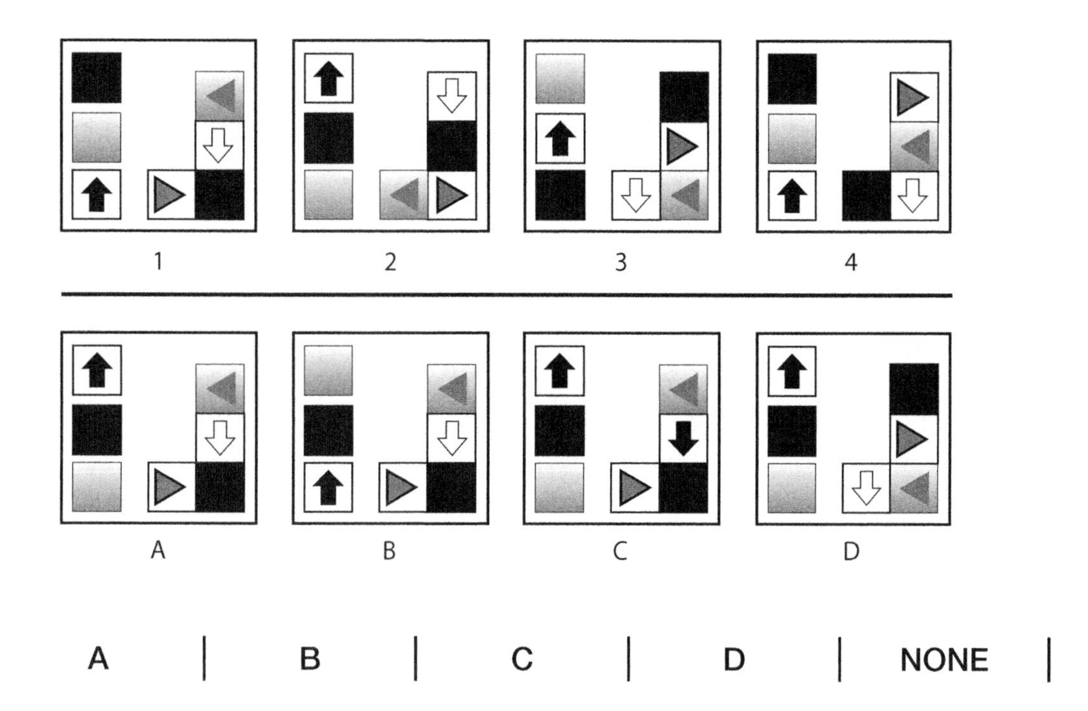

| A | B | C | D | NONE |

Q6. Which figure comes next in the series?

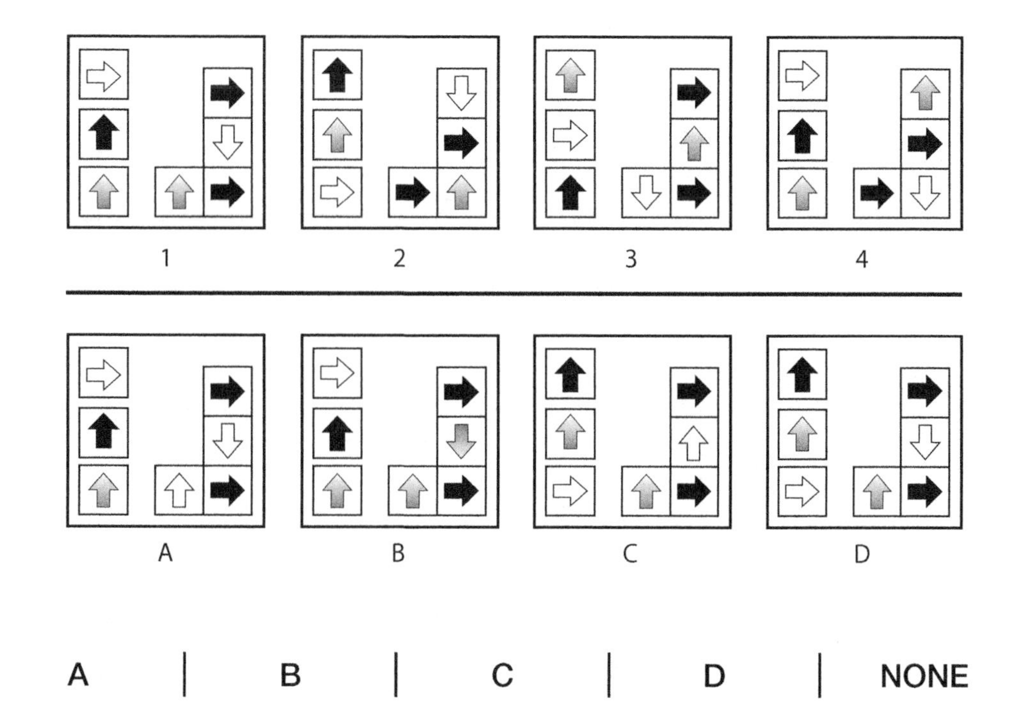

| A | B | C | D | NONE |

Q7. Which figure comes next in the series?

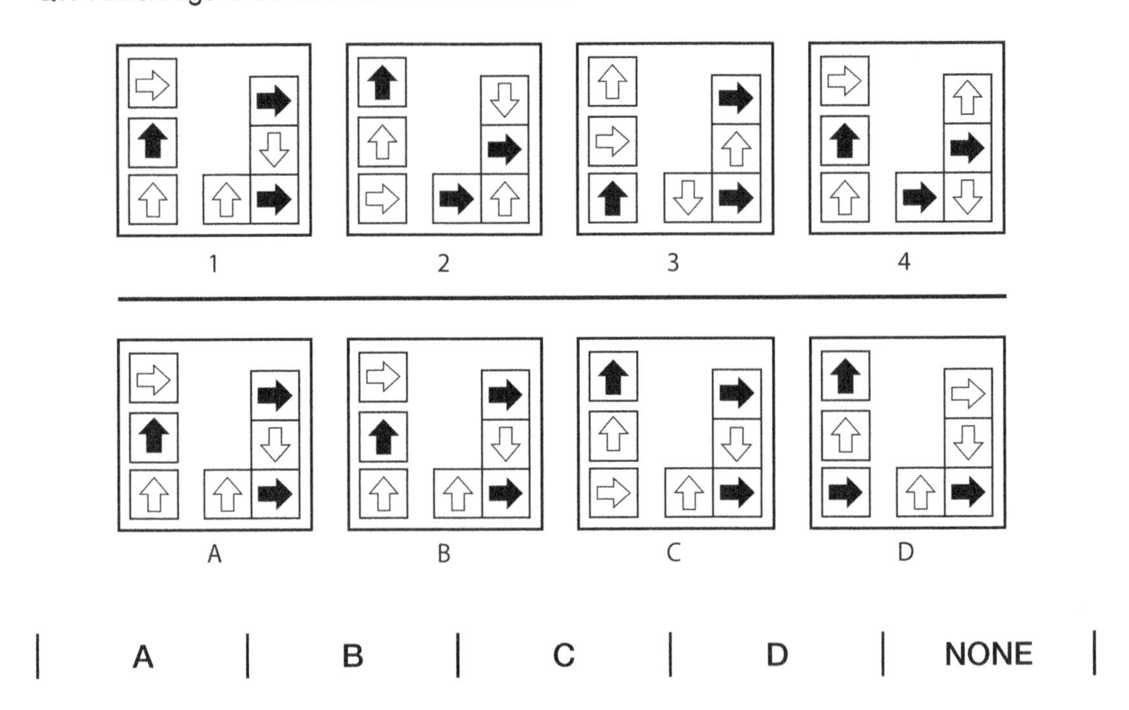

A	B	C	D	NONE

Q8. Which figure comes next in the series?

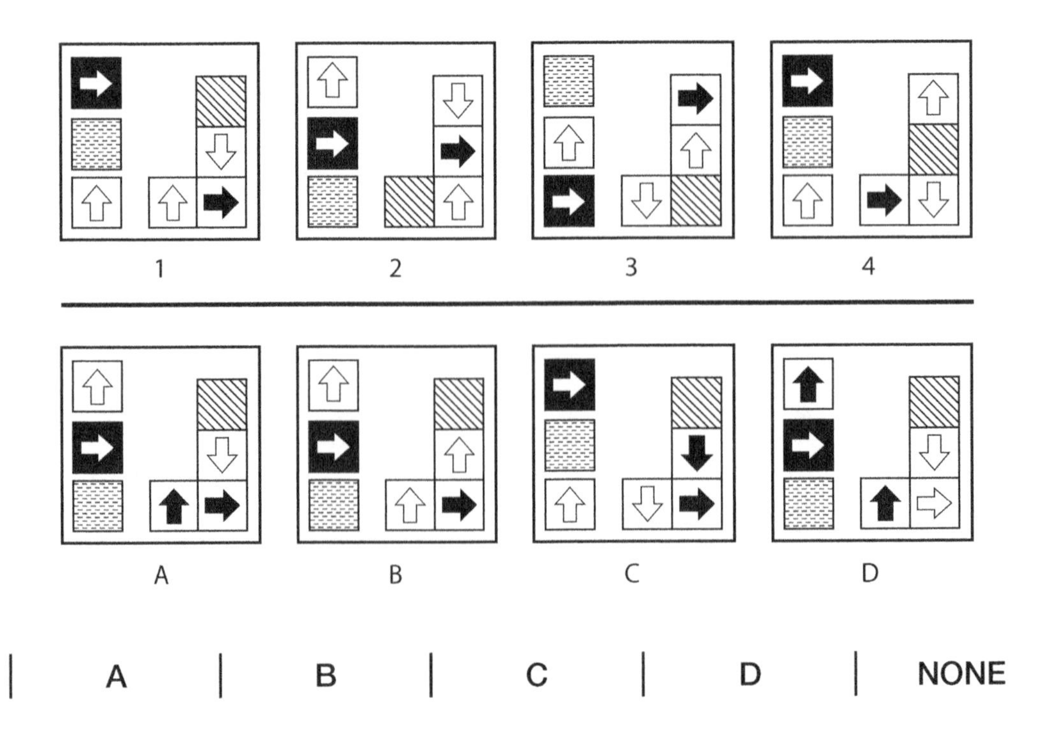

A	B	C	D	NONE

Q9. Which figure comes next in the series?

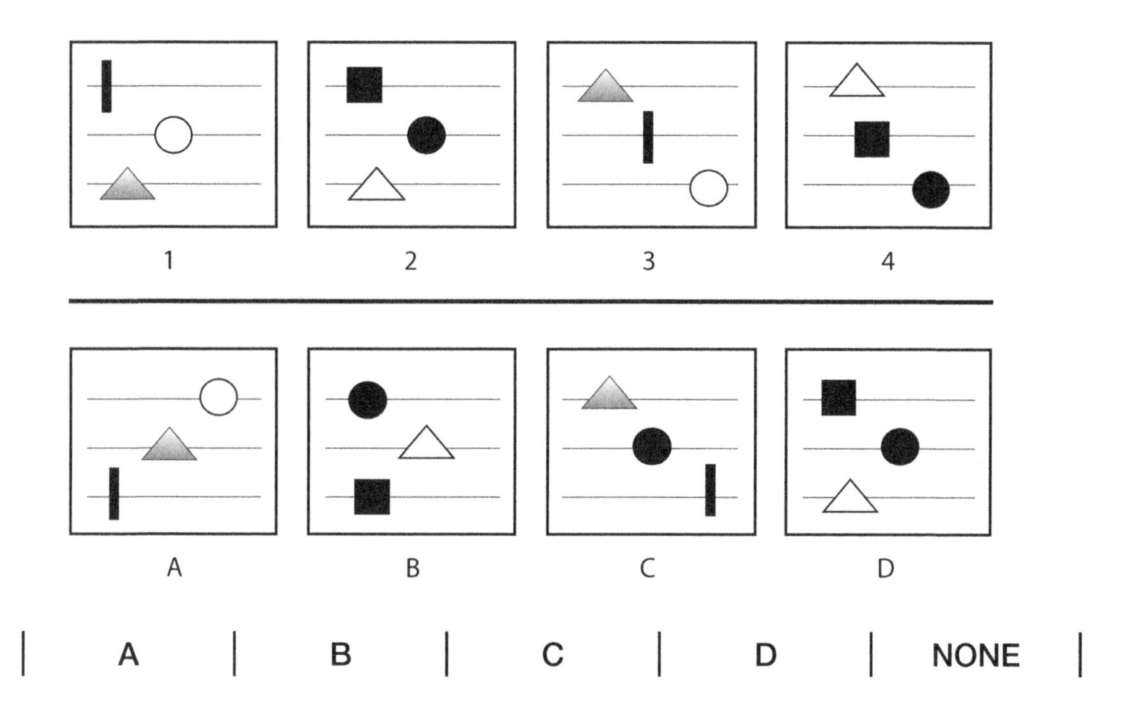

Q10. Which figure comes next in the series?

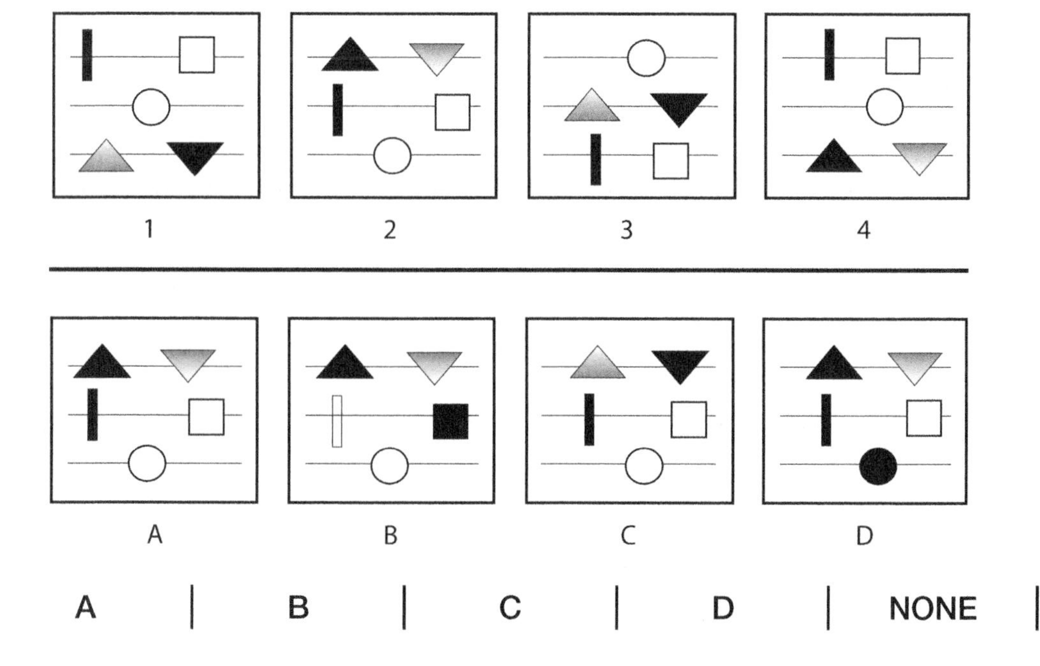

ANSWERS TO PRACTICE TESTS 3

Q1. B

Within each square of the series, the 3 squares to the left move down one as the sequence progresses.

Within each square of the series, the 4 shapes to the right move down one as the sequence progresses.

Q2. D

Within each square of the series, the 3 squares to the left move down one as the sequence progresses.

Within each square of the series, the 4 shapes to the right move down one as the sequence progresses.

Q3. C

Within each square of the series, the 3 squares to the left move up one as the sequence progresses.

Within each square of the series, the 4 shapes to the right move down one as the sequence progresses.

Q4. C

Within each square of the series, the 3 squares to the left move down one as the sequence progresses.

Within each square of the series, the 4 shapes to the right move up one as the sequence progresses.

Q5. A

Within each square of the series, the 3 squares to the left move down one as the sequence progresses.

Within each square of the series, the 4 shapes to the right move up one as the sequence progresses.

Q6. D

Within each square of the series, the 3 squares to the left move up one as the sequence progresses.

Within each square of the series, the 4 shapes to the right move up one as the sequence progresses.

Q7. C

Within each square of the series, the 3 squares to the left move up one as the sequence progresses.

Within each square of the series, the 4 shapes to the right move up one as the sequence progresses.

Q8. NONE

Within each square of the series, the 3 squares to the left move down one as the sequence progresses.

Within each square of the series, the 4 shapes to the right move up one as the sequence progresses.

Q9. A

Within each odd square (square 1 and 3), the shapes are moving down each line as the sequence progresses.

Within the even squares (square 2 and 4), the shapes are moving down each line as the sequence progresses.

Q10. C

Within each square the shapes are moving down each line as the sequence progresses. Once they reach the bottom they go back to the top. However, you will notice that the two triangular shapes alternate colours, switching from black to grey and vice versa, as the sequence progresses.

A FEW FINAL WORDS

You have now reached the end of the guide and no doubt you will be ready to start preparing for the Army Officer selection process. Before you go off and start on your preparation, consider the following.

The majority of candidates who pass the selection process have a number of common factors. These are as follows:

1. They believe in themselves.

The first factor is self-belief. Regardless of what anyone tells you, you can pass the AOSB and you can achieve high scores. Just like any job of this nature, you have to be prepared to work hard in order to be successful. The biggest piece of advice we can give you is to concentrate on matching the assessable qualities that form part of the scoring criteria. These should be at the forefront of your mind when going through the selection process. Make sure you have the self-belief to pass the selection process and fill your mind with positive thoughts.

2. They prepare fully.

The second factor is preparation. Those people who achieve in life prepare fully for every eventuality and that is what you must do when you apply to become an Officer with the Army. Work very hard and especially concentrate on your weak areas. Within this guide we have spoken a lot about preparation. Identify the areas that you are weak on and go all out to improve them.

3. They persevere.

Perseverance is a fantastic word. Everybody comes across obstacles or setbacks in their life, but it is what you do about those setbacks that is important. If you fail at something, then ask yourself 'why' have I failed? This will allow you to improve for next time and if you keep improving and trying, success will eventually follow. Apply this same method of thinking when you apply to join the Army as an Officer.

4. They are self-motivated.

How much do you want to join the Army? Do you want it, or do you really want it? When you apply to join you should want it more than anything in the world. Your levels of self motivation will shine through when you walk into the AFCO and when you attend the Army Officer Selection Board. For the weeks and months leading up to the selection process, be motivated as best as you can and always keep your fitness levels up as this will serve to increase your levels of motivation.

Work hard, stay focused, and secure your dream career.

The how2become team

The How2Become Team

WHY NOT TAKE A LOOK AT OUR OTHER ARMY GUIDES!

FOR MORE INFORMATION ON OUR ARMY GUIDES, PLEASE CHECK OUT THE FOLLOWING:

WWW.HOW2BECOME.COM